THE SOCIAL PSYCHOLOGY OF RACE RELATIONS

THE SOCIAL PSYCHOLOGY OF RACE RELATIONS

Leonard Bloom
Fellow of Sussex University

London   George Allen & Unwin Ltd
Ruskin House   Museum Street

First published in 1971

ISBN 0 04 301047 *cloth*
301041 5 *paper*

Printed in Great Britain
in 11 point Baskerville type
by Billing & Sons Limited
Guildford and London

'Probably a realization of no single fact is of such crucial significance for an understanding of racial antagonism as that the phenomenon had its rise only in modern times. . . . Our hypothesis is that racial exploitation and race prejudice developed among Europeans with the rise of capitalism and nationalism, and that because of the world-wide ramifications of capitalism, all racial antagonisms can be traced to the policies and attitudes of the leading capitalist people, the white people of Europe and North America.'
O. C. Cox, *Caste, Class and Race*, 1959

'. . . It would seem that nations still obey their immediate passions far more readily than their interests. Their interests serve them, at the best, as rationalizations for their passions; they parade their interests as their justification for satisfying their passions. Actually, why the national units should disdain, detest, abhor one another, and *that* even when they are at peace, is indeed a mystery. . . . It is just as though when it becomes a question of a number of people . . . all individual moral requirements were obliterated, and only the most primitive, the oldest, the crudest mental attitudes were left.'
Freud, *Reflections upon War and Death*, 1915

Acknowledgements

Most books are written by a committee – the author and those of his friends whose comments and suggestions encouraged him. This book is no exception. I deeply appreciate those who often took considerable trouble to assist me to clarify an argument, enliven my style, or most important, to stimulate me when the creative urge was feebler than usual.

But some friends have been particularly generous in their help, encouragement and interest, and I should be churlish if I failed to mention them. Much of whatever is reasonable in this little book is due to debate and discussion with them; the faults I hold myself responsible for.

Foremost, Professor George Westby, whose guidance lost nothing in the five thousand miles between his office in Cardiff and mine in Lusaka. My thanks are also offered to my friends Mordecai Betera, Moddie-Guy Chongo, Fred Dube, Rogers Kasongamulilo, Les and Gesse Martin, Livingston Mqotsi and Ernest Shenton. They have all helped me far more than they knew.

Lusaka – London

Contents

Introduction

It is the argument of this book that race relations and race attitudes 'are the social products of the life of a group whose individual members have all been exposed to the same kind of psycho-social environment. . . . As a social habit, the attitude has a history; it testifies to the continuity of the present with the past in the life of the group.' (MacCrone, 1937.) Race relations and race attitudes are not fundamentally different from other human behaviour, for example, political or religious beliefs and practice, and they are learned through similar processes. Although race attitudes often have an irrational component, they are equally often meaningful if they are related to their historical and socio-economic context.

It follows that if conditions be changed, and if individual fears and anxieties be eliminated or reduced, the intensity of disruptive behaviour such as prejudice and discrimination can be mitigated.

The discussion will, then, begin with a description and analysis of the scientific relevance of race to understanding human behaviour, and of the manner in which myths and unscientific beliefs have accumulated. Next follow psychological and social accounts, and their relation to personality and to family background. But the individual lives within a network of economic, social and political influences, which provide constraints and encouragements for his racial (and other) beliefs and relationships. To illustrate the interdependence of social and psychological factors, and to show that they can only be meaningfully analysed within a historical context, two differing areas, Southern Africa and Great Britain, are analysed. Finally, the contribution of social psychology to our understanding of how *new* patterns of racial relationships may be generated is assessed.

Throughout the book it is accepted that what men have learned they can unlearn, but this does not imply any complacency about the difficulties encountered in attempting to order society and individuals so that the violence of their irrational beliefs may be modified.

Chapter 1

THE MYTH AND THE
MEANING OF RACE

I. INTRODUCTION

The major biological variations of mankind are as natural as
deposits of minerals, and like those deposits, they are ignored
or exploited as men think profitable. It is paradoxical that the
biological variations of mankind are quite irrelevant to his
future welfare, whilst they have become dangerously and
irrelevantly interpreted and evaluated in the light of destructive myths. On a purely biological level it matters little whether
Australia stays white or not; but on a social and political level,
this issue determines all others.

The *meaning* of race has become subordinate to the *myth* of
race: it is politically and socially profitable to emphasize the
biological differences of mankind, and to minimize (or to deny)
the biologically more important universality. Memmi (1964),
in a discussion of the nature of racialism, makes the point that
when the protagonist of race differences insists upon the differences between races he is seeking to justify the exclusion of one
race from humanity: he seeks to create strangers. If there are
no biological differences between the groups, he will invent
them (as Nazi ideologists invented quite imaginary differences
between 'Aryans' and Jews); if there are differences, he will
exaggerate them and interpret them to his profit.

This chapter is therefore an attempt to distinguish the
scientific reality of race from the accretion of mythical interpretations of race differences. It does not seek to deny that race
exists; it does offer evidence to support the argument that race
is never a satisfactory explanation of human behaviour.

II. THE SCIENTIFIC MEANING OF 'RACE'

As a species *homo sapiens* has not a particularly venerable history.
Most authorities date the family of modern man at about a

million years. But psychologists are less concerned with the origins of mankind than they are with the consequences of the persistence with which modern man during the past three centuries has interested himself in interpreting and evaluating the similarities and differences between human groups: favouring some similarities and differences, and rejecting and condemning others. An obvious difference between human groups is 'race', and considerable human ingenuity (and misguided effort) has been wasted on the attempt to define races and their characteristics and to derive social policies from the claimed findings.

Race, scientifically, is a biological term and is narrowly confined to the bodily characteristics that distinguish one group of humans from another. It says nothing about any psychological or social characteristics, nor does it imply any judgement about the 'inferiority' or 'superiority' of any race.

> 'Race . . . is a major segment of a species, originally occupying, since the first dispersal of mankind, a large, geographically unified, and distinct region, and touching on territories of other races only by relatively narrow corridors. Within such a region each race acquired its distinctive genetic attributes – both its visible physical appearance and its invisible biological properties – through the selective forces of all aspects of the environment, including culture.' (Coon, 1966.)

However, whatever might have been the original geographical and genetic isolation, there has been no 'pure' race since the earliest prehistoric times, because the history of mankind has been a constant wandering and racial fusion. Increasingly during the last few thousand years, the mixture of races has become irreversible and any rigid classification is bound to be arbitrary.

The most favoured and moderate view is that there are five major human races: European (or Caucasoid), African (or Negroid), Asiatic (or Mongoloid), American Indian and Australoid, but even within these broad groups, geneticists find no difficulty in teasing out sub-races resulting from mankind's continual migration. The Australian Aborigines were once thought to be an almost uniquely insulated group, but they are now thought to be migrants originating somewhere in the South Pacific, possibly Java, and therefore having links with the main stream of human biological development (Mulvaney, 1966).

But Europe is possibly the best example of the intricacy of mixture of different types, as Boas (1966) has well illustrated. The Celts swept across Italy from Western Europe to Asia Minor; the Teutonic tribes wandered from the Black Sea to Spain, Italy and North Africa; Slavs moved northwards across Russia, and south into the Balkans; the Moors occupied a large part of Spain; the Roman and Greek slaves were absorbed by the host population, and Roman colonization influenced much of the Mediterranean. In more recent times Turks, Greeks and Italians, Africans and West Indians are among the many strains present in Western Europe, and an already inextricably mixed population is becoming even more mixed.

Indeed, if the populations of any continent are analysed historically, it is impossible to do more than to surmise what the original (and changing) groups might be. Even the Negroid (African) race, which is often claimed to have the most pronounced physical characteristics, displays wide internal differences. The African race includes both the tallest and the shortest of mankind; there are very dark people from Central Africa, and the light-complexioned Sotho who are no darker than many Mediterranean peoples; some Africans have 'Caucasoid' features; not all Africans have tightly curled hair. And if we try to associate Negroid characteristics with blood groups, immunity from or susceptibility to certain diseases, the relationship between genetic, racial and socio-cultural factors is so involved and fraught with so many uncertainties that only a writer resolutely resolved to advocate purely genetic factors would be bold enough to do so.

However races be described or delineated, they form populations that have all diverged from a common human stock, and they all belong to a common species. Although physical differences like skin colour are obvious, and less obvious differences such as blood groupings and predisposition to certain diseases exist, all humans have the same genetic and constitutional qualities. All races can breed with other races, and no disadvantages have arisen from such interbreeding as far back as historical research can discover.

B

The interest in race classification is recent and is closely linked with political (rather than scientific) considerations. The wide disagreements about the number and definition of races suggest how arbitrary and subjective is the nature of race classification. Gossett (1965) lists in detail the varying numbers of races that have been suggested since this interest developed. For example:

> 'Linnaeus had found four human races; Blumenbach had five . . . Burke had sixty-three . . . Haeckel had thirty-six . . . Beniker had seventeen races and thirty types. Jean Finot, one of the critics of race theorizing, concluded . . . "We must bless Heaven for having preserved us from a thousand million races and consequent classification." '

A moderate conclusion is that despite the shortage of historical-biological data about the earlier periods of human existence, it is clear that broad categories of mankind can be distinguished on the basis of appearance and blood groupings, but that there has been so much mixture of races, and therefore so much modifiability of these physical qualities, that it is of little use in understanding human behaviour or history to analyse them in terms of physical race. Humans have shown extraordinary physical adaptation to their physical environment, and an insatiable desire to migrate, and the 'progress made by man, in any field, seems to have been increasingly, if not exclusively, based on culture and the transmission of cultural achievements and not on the transmission of genetic endowment'. (UNESCO, 1965.)

Regardless of the scientific opinion that there are no valid grounds to attribute to race any serious role in human history, racial beliefs are nevertheless real to many men and women, and mythical beliefs about race are commonly held. The two most persistent myths are that race and culture are directly related, and that some races are intellectually superior.

III. RACE AND CULTURE

There is no direct connection between race and culture. Nations and states, language and culture, are the products of history and cannot be understood apart from a study of their internal development and external relations. Moreover, the fantastic social and technological developments of the last five hundred years have occurred within far too short a time for any genetic changes to have taken place, and are spreading throughout the world far too rapidly for genetic factors to have any influence.

Possibly the most striking example of rapid cultural change is the modern history of Japan, which has developed from feudalism to modern industrialism in barely a century. The development of Africa since about the late 1940s or early 1950s illustrates the same point. For example, Zambia became an independent state on 24 October 1964, and within a few months a university was founded, education was greatly extended and the Development Plan inaugurated a rapid urbanization-industrialization. The culture of pre-independence was well on the way to far-reaching modernization. Did the inhabitants of Zambia one day in 1964 become suddenly fitted genetically to share the achievements of the technology of the Western world, when they were not so fitted before? The only change was in the social and political status and organization of Zambia.

In addition, the degree of racial homogeneity or heterogeneity within a state or nation or culture area is a very wide-ranging variable. The USA is an excellent example of how a nation-state has developed with possibly the most racially mixed population of any nation, and South Africa will develop similar racial diversity within political unity, despite the artificial barriers of *apartheid*. Even the tiny state of Zambia has a population drawn from all races, shares three cultural streams and yet shows every sign of becoming as stable and as mixed a state as Switzerland.

Neither does race determine language. A Frenchman might be of Caucasoid stock, but he might be a Negro from Chad, or a Lebanese, or an Arab from Tunis, or even an Annamite from Indo-China who had been brought up as a Catholic and educated in a French school. Apart from their physical appearances, these people would be indistinguishable in their culture and values from metropolitan Frenchmen. A man in appearance African might be a third-generation inhabitant of Cardiff, and speak in a flat Cardiff accent with only the slightest hint of a Jamaican lilt. Or he might be an English-speaking Sotho from Johannesburg, unable to communicate directly with an equally African-looking man from the Congo who only speaks French and Lovale.

There is, in short, so much variation in government and law, social, religious and political beliefs, economic organization, art and music, language (and other elements of culture) within any race, that it is chasing a rainbow to find a specific culture for a specific race.

As communication and transportation develop, the inventions, beliefs and values of different peoples will all the more easily spread to regions even at opposite ends of the earth. There is no reason why the habit of *homo sapiens* of adopting what pleases or suits him of a foreign culture should cease.

IV. RACE AND INTELLECTUAL CAPACITY

There is no more reason to link race and intellectual capacity than to link race and culture. Every individual is born with a certain heredity: a potential which is dependent upon his familial genes and not upon his race. Whether this potential is fully or only partially realized depends upon his individual experience, and particularly upon what is offered him by his culture and education. His society can encourage him to use his potential abilities to the utmost, or the burden of discouragement may be so heavy that he is little activated to excel. The proportion of eminence and mediocrity is much the same in all societies; but each society makes use of these in different ways and to different extents.

The belief that there are races that are mentally superior and others that are inferior is both scientifically wrong and highly persistent. There seems every reason to reject arguments that seek to prove that a particular race is 'primitive' or less capable than others of adopting a high level of technological skill.

The term 'primitive' is, itself, used rarely and then with circumspection by anthropologists. Lévi-Strauss (1963) comments that

'. . . attempts to explain alleged differences between the so-called primitive mind and scientific thought have resorted to qualitative differences between the working processes of the mind in both cases, while assuming that the entities which they were studying remained very much the same. . . . The difference lies, not in the quality of the intellectual process, but in the nature of the things to which it is applied.'

Man thinks equally well – or badly – in all cultures. But he thinks well or badly about different things. The power of man's mind has probably not changed since *homo sapiens* evolved. What *has* changed has been the continual enlargement of areas to which these powers have been applied. There may well be living in the Kalahari a man or woman with the potential ability of an Einstein. But his ability will be employed in tasks that *in the terms of our scientific culture* are unskilled and 'inferior'. Indeed it could be plausibly argued that it requires exceptional ability to survive in the rigorous and (to us) most inhospitable and dangerous environment in which the Bushman succeeds in surviving physically and creating a social system, morality and art.[1]

Once the testing of intelligence by standardized techniques became widely employed during World War I, there seemed to be a scientific means to compare the intellectual abilities of races. But the testing of intelligence between different race or cultural groups has failed to disclose any group differences that cannot be attributed to social factors, and the possibility that there *are* race differences is still unproven. Testing over the past half-century or so is almost unanimous in supporting the view that there are no grounds to claim that any one race is innately superior (or inferior) in intellectual ability to any other. One of the few recent reports that claims to find race differences is the massive analysis of Shuey (1966), in which

[1] For systematic elaborations of the view that the intellectual processes of 'primitive' or non-literate people are fundamentally as logical – and as illogical – as those of literate peoples, see, for example, Boas, F., *The Mind of Primitive Man*, New York, The Free Press, 1965; Radin, P., *Primitive Man as Philosopher*, New York, Dover, 1957; Tempels, P., 'Bantu Philosophy', *Présence Africaine*, Paris, 1959; Thomas, L.-V., *Les idéologies Negro-Africaines d'Aujourd'hui*, Université de Dakar, 1965; N'Daw, A., 'Peut-on parler d'une pensée Africaine?' *Présence Africaine*.

qualified approval is given to investigations that claim to relate intelligence to race, but Shuey's interpretation of the research she discusses has been seriously questioned by other psychologists. (See *Contemporary Psychology*, February 1967.)

The controversy about the relationship of race to intelligence has recently been aroused once more by Jensen (1969) in the USA, and by Burt *et al.* (1970) in the UK. Jensen's meticulously detailed argument goes directly to the heart of educational and social policy, for, having dealt with the question 'How much can we boost IQ and scholastic achievement?' he continues by examining the causes for the (to him) disappointing results of some compensatory educational programmes.

Jensen begins by giving the term 'intelligence' a rather specific meaning: 'it is probably best thought of as a capacity for abstract reasoning and problem solving', because, he argues, this capacity is most closely connected with the needs of our society's educational and occupational systems. It is possible to argue to the contrary that this definition already assumes that this *social* definition of intelligence is so specific and clear that it could *logically* be related to genetic determinants of behaviour, there are few pieces of social behaviour (if any) that can directly be related to this or that genetic mechanism. Certainly so fluctuating a concept as intelligence, which relates to *learned* behaviour, cannot be reduced to the same sort of genetic argument as, say, eye colour.

Jensen, however, proceeds to examine intelligence and concludes that even if one makes all allowances for such environmental factors as membership of a social class, the genetic factors are far more important than the environmental in determining intelligence. The role of the environment, he argues, is little more than a 'threshold variable': 'extreme environmental deprivation can keep the child from performing up to his genetic potential, but an enriched educational programme cannot push the child above that potential'. It follows that the enriched educational programmes fail because they are based on a supposition that intelligence is mainly the result of environmental differences. The correct procedure, Jensen believes, is that education should be made rewarding for the different patterns of children's ability. In itself this is an unobjectionable proposal, but it becomes objectionable if it is employed unscientifically to support a political view which favours differential educations for children or different social classes or races, *simply because* they are of different social class or race. Moreover, there is no scientific ground offered by Jensen to minimize the right of every child to live in a society in which he or she does not begin life with a social disadvantage, in terms of the criteria of intelligence that are devised to suit a predominantly middle-class educational and occupational system.

The tendency of the criticisms of the objections to Jensen's gross overemphasis upon genetic factors is well expressed by Miller (1970), who draws attention to the pervasive and often lasting influence of the very early environment on later performance: 'environmental inadequacy is the primary factor leading to progressive intellectual retardation and the inability to cope effectively in an increasingly complex society.' The environmental cycle of defeat–failure–defeat from parents' to child's generation must be broken at least as early as three years of age. The Council of the Society for the Psychological Study of Social Issues, which is composed of psychologists throughout the USA, has issued a statement which points out how seriously open to criticism are Jensen's psychological and genetic arguments, and observes that the major failure of so-called compensatory education has been in its execution, size and scope, and not its underlying philosophy. Moreover, where specific skills are taught in well-designed programmes, then these programmes have been effective. (See Deutsch, 1969.)

It must be admitted that group differences in the average scores on intelligence tests do occur, and that minority groups often *on the average* score lower than members of the majority group. In the USA for example, Negroes, Puerto Ricans, Mexicans and Portuguese have tested below the white average (see, e.g., Dreger & Miller, 1960; Lesser *et al.*, 1965). The causes of these group differences are, by most modern psychologists, attributed to socio-psychological factors, and the differences between races are paralleled by similar differences between social classes. George de Vos (1967), for example, analysed group differences between the Burakumin caste in Japan and the majority group, and found that the Burakumin had a lower *average*, tested intelligence score than other Japanese. They are all Japanese and, therefore, of the same race, and de Vos suggests that the mere fact of belonging to a group with pariah status has deleterious consequences for the individual's intellectual functioning.

There are four main reasons why the comparison of intelligence tests of different race groups is unreliable:

1. *Socio-economic background.* The cultural deprivation of those from a lower socio-economic class is more pervasive and enduring than a comparison confined to schooling alone would suggest (see Passow, 1965). In the USA programmes such as 'Head Start' are now under way to remedy the cultural and educational poverty of slum children, and Gray and Klaus (1965) have found that children who attended a summer school with special training programmes designed to encourage and motivate rather than to offer formal schooling, persistently showed higher scores in intelligence testing than children in similar social circumstances who did not attend such camps. Riessman (1962, 1964) has studied the culturally deprived child and he concludes that for deprived children, not only is the school or learning culture inadequate, it is irrelevant, because there is little in their lives to make them *want* to be concerned with intellectual activity, education and fitting themselves for the predominantly middle-class values of their society.

2. *Schooling.* There is considerable evidence to show that intelligence test scores are influenced by the length and the quality of schooling. One investigation concludes that migrant, Negro children who began their schooling in Philadelphia were inferior on three tests to the Philadelphia-born children, but by the time they had reached the sixth grade they had caught up (Lee, 1951). This factor is of major important because much of the testing of intelligence has failed to point out that it is often the minority race groups who attend the poorer schools. For instance, in South Africa the *per capita* annual expenditure in African schools is about £6 10s, and that in white schools about £56 (Horrell, 1965), and similar comparisons have been observed in the USA, particularly in the South. Less directly obvious than the results of financial poverty of school pro-

grammes is the effect on motivation of schools in which equipment and teaching are inadequate, classes overcrowded and buildings unattractive and old-fashioned. Another depressing factor is the effect of absence of models of success which could show that achievement is rewarding, and the ignorance of the vocational and educational opportunities that are available. Poor schooling entails a restricted view of the community and the place of the student within it.

3. *Language.* Many tests are based upon language, and it is rare that a minority group has a complete facility in the language of the majority group. There is, for example, evidence that West Indian children immigrant to the UK, who speak English as their native language, are at a disadvantage because they are speaking an English that has evolved many of its own linguistic characteristics. Even the American Negro, who grows up in an English language environment, is handicapped in that, because of his general cultural poverty, he often uses and hears English of an inferior kind, spoken by adults with less language facility than the average white. When non-linguistic performance tests are administered, the average score of those with a linguistic handicap is higher.

4. *Motivation.* There is no reason why all subjects should be equally interested in testing, and equally concerned to do their best. There is no reason why all subjects should equally trust the tester and be equally relaxed in the test situation. Hopi children, for example, do poorly on tests because of the prohibition in their culture on competition: if *you* do well then your friend will be shamed. Among Australian subjects, and among some Negro groups, it has been found that subjects were reluctant to work fast and to keep to the time of the test, because they were anxious to work with care and do their best. They were anxious about their ability in the test situation and felt that they would do better by working slowly. Consequently they scored lower than they might had they worked faster. Even the race of the tester influences the test results. Athey *et al.* (1960) have shown that the answers Negroes give to Negro interviewers differ from those given to white interviewers, being distorted in the direction of reticence and caution in a situation in which the white interviewer is perceived as representative of

a critical authority. *Where anxiety is provoked and suspicion aroused, performance often deteriorates.*[1]

In brief, before we could conclude that race differences in mental capacity existed, we should have to meet the following conditions, which have never been met satisfactorily in any investigation:[2]

'There must be equal *opportunities* for the individuals of both groups . . . to participate freely . . . in the prevailing currents of benefits and progress of the large community to which the groups belong. . . . There must be similar *incentives* to master learning, significant for the real life of the individuals. . . . There must be similar group *expectancy* and opportunities for *goal-setting* in the home and community.' (Long, 1957.)

If all allowances are made, therefore, for cultural, social and motivational conditions, the evidence for the intellectual superiority of any race dwindles to insignificance.[3]

V. RACE RELATIONS AND RACE IDEOLOGY

It should be clear by now that much of the notion of race is unscientific; but distorted or false notions are as interesting to

[1] Three recent studies slightly modify these findings: Sattler (1966) and Bryant *et al.* (1966) found 'moderate shifting'. Bryant *et al.* observed that Negroes were more accepting of white examiners than whites were of Negro examiners. See also Baratz (1967).

[2] Claims have occasionally been made that testing was carried out in areas where social and economic conditions *were* equal, and reference is often made to the Kent County studies of Tanser (1939). However, a psychologist born in Kent and educated there at the time at which the study was made gives descriptions of the area that make the claim of equality hardly tenable (see Smart, 1963).

[3] Other major analyses of the relationship of membership of a minority-disadvantaged group to intellectual or occupational performance include: Baxter B. (*et al.*), 'Job testing and the disadvantaged', *American Psychologist*, 1969, **24,** 7, 637–49; Craine, R. L., 'School integration and occupational achievement of Negroes', *Amer. J. Sociology*, 1970, **75,** 4 (part 2), 593–606; Gurin, P., 'Motivation and aspiration of Southern Negro College youth', 1970, **75,** 4 (part 2), 607–31. These, and other papers, emphasize how society affects motivation, which influences performance in its turn. In South Africa, Biesheuvel has pioneered the careful analysis of the varied influences on intelligence; e.g. Biesheuvel, S., and Liddicoat, R., 'The effects of cultural factors on intelligence-test performance', *J. Nat. Inst. Personnel Res.* 1959, **8,** 3–14.

the social psychologist as correct ones. For most purposes the concept of race that determines or justifies policies and programmes is social, and is in response to supposed pressures or needs. Attributes of a race are assumed because a society *needs* to assume their truth. Race is defined functionally, and race relations, prejudice and conflict are firmly rooted in the functioning of a society and frequently form an integral part of its system of values.

From this point of view

'race is a human grouping which is *culturally* defined in a given society. This grouping is considered different from other groupings similarly defined by virtue of innate and visible physical characteristics. In the extreme case these groupings are considered, rightly or wrongly, as biologically separate sub-groups.' (Van den Berghe, 1958.)

Banton (1966) quotes a neat and still pertinent illustration of race as a social category, and also shows how race and social status can be identified.

'An English traveller in early 19th-century Brazil enquired of a coloured Brazilian whether a certain high official was not a mulatto only to be told "He was, but he is not now". When the traveller queried this, the Brazilian turned the tables on him by posing the rhetorical question *"Can a Capitamór* be a mulatto?"'

Negroes are presumably genetically similar in the South of the USA, the North of the USA, South Africa, Brazil and Trinidad. But in social terms they are highly dissimilar. They are perceived and treated variously by whites in these areas, and they perceive themselves variously. A striking illustration of the cultural-social definition of a race is given by the history of the Japanese and Arabs in South Africa during the past twenty years, since the present government came into office.

Before 1962 there were never more than about fifty Japanese living in South Africa, mostly diplomats living in Pretoria. In 1961–2, the government began negotiations to increase trade with Japan, Japanese businessmen came to South Africa, and in 1962 a team of Olympic swimmers arrived. The Japanese were the same biological race at the end of 1961 as they were at the beginning, but in November 1961, for many purposes they had 'white status' conferred upon them and were classified as 'other Asiatics'. Rapidly known as 'pig-iron whites', the Japanese found their conferred status inconsistent and anomalous. They were still subject to provisions of the Immorality Act, and were legally excluded from some public amenities but not from others.

In May 1961 questions were raised about the Arabs who had settled about seventy years earlier on the Bluff, Durban. There were many doubts about their history, but the general belief was that they had been shipwrecked. During the seventy years they had married Africans, yet spoke a distinct non-African language and followed some Muslim customs. Initially they were classified as Africans (because of their appearance, possibly), then they were reclassified as Coloured. Later it was decided to classify them as 'other Asiatics' and move them to an area allocated to Indians.

VI. THE SOCIAL FUNCTION OF RACIAL MYTHS

Do these racial beliefs have any function, or are they as irrational as the history of the Durban Arabs suggest? Nash (1962) has stressed four main functions:

1. They provide a moral justification for maintaining a society in which one group is deprived of rights and privileges. They thereby permit the dominant group to reconcile Christian or humanitarian (or other) ideals with the so-called 'practical' values. The South African Group Areas legislation is morally justifiable to South African whites, because it enables those of a like race to live together. This deflects possible concern from a policy that enables speculative developers to purchase desirable land at artificially low prices.

2. They discourage the subordinate groups from attempting to improve their status or to try to change the society, by equating racialism with the very foundations of the society. A change in the practice of racialism is equated with the destruction of the total social order.

3. They provide a cause to which political action can be allied, and are particularly potent in focusing economic and social uncertainty on to a specific threat.

4. They justify the existing economic situation, and permit the argument that it should not be changed in the future, because to change will mean poverty for the masses and lower living standards for the dominant groups. But this argument is often expressed more palatably – if more speciously – in the converse.

Cecil Rhodes, for example, in a speech to the Chartered Company in 1892, of which Mr Pecksniff might have been proud, said:

> 'The idea that the taking up of the uncivilized portions of the world is to the advantage of the classes is erroneous; the proceeding is entirely to the advantage of the masses. . . . The classes could spend their money under any flag, but the poor masses had no money to spend on these speculations – these gold and silver mines. . . .' ('Imperialist', 1897.)

Nash argues that a racial ideology grows and becomes a central feature of the value-system of a society in times of social crisis or conflict, or when a dominant group perceives its dominance (economic, social and political) to be threatened by a subordinate group. A group that is psychologically secure has little need for the spurious defences of a racial ideology to persuade itself of the stability – and justice – of its position of dominance.

Race ideologies and patterns of race relations are the result of a society's economic and social history and operate, therefore, within a given socio-economic system, and it is not necessary to be a Marxist to agree with Haldane (1961), who described the manner in which racial beliefs serve to stabilize a society in which there are class differentiations and marked economic inequality.

It is equally important to appreciate that caste and class ideologies and relations are closely similar to race ideologies and relations, and groups cleave to their superior class or caste status as tenaciously as they cleave to race distinctions.

The hostility for example between French- and English-speaking Canadians, while related to economic and political conflicts, has endured for more than one hundred years, and is as bitter and as violent as an avowedly racial conflict. Dedijer (1966) in his study of the last few days of the Hapsburg

Empire, devotes two chapters which demonstrate with poignant clarity how the political and social conflicts between the various peoples of the empire were violent, brutal and psychologically in no way different from openly racial antagonisms. He quotes a folk-song of the repressed Serbians:

'Krajina's like a blood-soaked rag;
Blood is our fare at noon, blood still at evening.
On every lip is the taste of blood,
With never a peaceful day or any rest.'

The 'primitive rebels of Bosnia' responded to their persecution by developing an intense nationalism, with which was associated an active interest in intellectual and cultural activities. And more recently the relationship between Afrikaans and English-speaking whites in South Africa, that had the intensity of racialism a half-century ago, has been transformed into the non-racial but none the less bitter and intransigent struggle for economic, political and social power.

Many social psychologists therefore have tended to discuss minority–majority group situations rather than race. Race relations have become subordinated to more general questions of contact between groups where there is conflict. It matters little to the psychologist whether the groups do, or do not, perceive each other as belonging to different races or social classes. The essential element is that one group singles out another group, and one of them is dominant, enjoying higher social status and greater privileges and power. The other is subordinate and excluded from full participation in the society. Members of both the dominant and the subordinate groups normally are proscribed by law and by custom from moving into the other, and their roles and status are ascribed to members, regardless of personal merit or demerit, qualities and potentials.

Minority–majority situations do not depend upon mere numbers. In South Africa, the 25% of the population that is white is the effective majority. The question of majority–minority group relations arises when there is a conflict about social and economic power, and this is usually gravest when it is combined with a consciousness of race differences, that is, when there is group dissatisfaction with the status pattern of the society *and* there are the elements of race antipathies.

A consequence of this broad conception is that an individual can belong to more than one socially defined group and can, therefore, enter into differing patterns of relationship. He is one person in one set of circumstances and another person in a different set. A medical doctor in South Africa has, qua doctor, a high status and is a member of a wealthy and influential élite. But if he is an African, an Indian or a Coloured doctor, he sinks to the status of 'non-white'. The writer was once asked by an incredulous Afrikaans youth, 'Can a Kaffir be a doctor?' The tension of reconciling incompatible or conflicting roles and their status can be psychologically damaging. But even more serious are the race attitudes associated with varying patterns of minority–majority group relations. Race attitudes are beliefs that an individual's race entails given psychological character-istics, together with favourable or critical feelings about these attributes. Moreover, an individual may have attitudes about *himself* qua member of a race, which are defined by the wider society and inculcated during his early childhood.

VII. THE STRUCTURE OF RACE ATTITUDES AND RACE RELATIONS

A recent attempt to relate the pattern of race relations to race attitudes and ideology is that of Rex (1970), who moves beyond the classical Marxist position of Cox (1959) to analyse situations that characterize the contemporary position of race relations in Western Europe and (to a large extent) the usa. The present situation is largely urban. A complex system of social and economic stratification prevents groups from inter-acting except for a limited number of purposes, for instance, at work. There are groups living in the same area who to a large extent form separate communities: that is, there is cultural and social pluralism. In these situations a specific group of those defined as outsiders or strangers performs roles and occupies a status that is considered inferior by the 'host' community: certain groups are defined as pariahs. Frequently the pariah group, being distinguishable, inferior and powerless, is the target for recrimination and blame in times of crisis: that is, the pariah is also a ready-made, defenceless, scapegoat. Thus race conflict is inseparably intertwined with social-economic class conflicts.

Rex insists that an essential element of the race relations situations that are of importance in our time is their ideology. The situations are rationalized, made plausible or legitimized, in terms of a system of beliefs or even of myths. The ideology both legitimizes the situation, and arises out of the pattern that the situation presents. The doctrine of the elect both provided a plausible justification for slavery, and arose out of the need to present the inequalities of slavery as God-given.

In order therefore to remedy a race relations situation it is necessary both to modify the structure of a society and its economic system, and to modify its ideology or systems of belief. It is significant that the militant black power movements appear to be focusing their attention on social issues that go beyond the narrow concern with black–white relationships, to a critical determination to modify the structure and beliefs of an international social system in which gross inequality is a characteristic.

Historically, race relations have polarized around two contrasting types, paternalistic and competitive (Van den Berghe, 1958), with differing psychological characteristics attributed to the majority and minority groups. The *paternalistic* system is essentially agricultural with a simple economic system, a wide gap between the living standards of the majority and minority groups, a small dominant minority, and no ideological conflict about the basis of the system. The division of labour is along strictly race lines. Everyone knows his place in the system and there is small reason in the economic organization to precipitate change. This resembles feudalism in Europe and was typical for nearly two hundred years of the relations between Xhosa and Europeans in the Cape until the late nineteenth century (Robertson, 1934, 1935). In this system prejudice is both intense and constant, the dominant group believing stereotypes of the subservient group to be childish and immature, uninhibited, impulsive, violent, inferior. There is a pseudo-tolerance, similar to the tolerance that one shows to a favourite animal, and acts of violent discipline alternate with acts of genuine affection. (This oscillation of mood, and its underlying ambivalence, is described unsentimentally in Olive Schreiner's *Story of an African Farm*, in a novel in which the authoress's insights about South Africa are still unrivalled.)

The attitudes of the dominant group are typically expressed in this extract from a contemporaneous eulogy of Cecil Rhodes. He had a

'great liking for, and sympathy with the black men, the natives of the country. . . . He had thousands of natives under him in the De Beers mines. . . . He was always looking after their interests . . . and his favourite recreation every Sunday afternoon was to go into the De Beers native compound . . . and throw in shillings for the natives to dive for. . . .

'Mr Rhodes is absolutely free from contempt for the black man. He looks upon him and treats him as a fellow-man, differing simply in his lower level of development. . . . He regards them as children, with something of pity in his affection for them, and he treats them like children, affectionately but firmly. . . .' ('Imperialist', 1897.)

The *competitive* system develops in a more sophisticated and urbanized economic system, as in modern South Africa, and the gap in living standards between the various groups partially overlaps, and is therefore not entirely along race lines. There is considerable mobility, as an industrial economy demands, and a complicated stratification within the majority and the minority groups. The status of the dominant group is constantly threatened by the pressure towards upward mobility of the subordinate group. For example, in South Africa the economic necessity for improving and extending African education has been complicated by openly expressed fears of the danger to the system of *apartheid* of an educated African population. There is often an ideological conflict, particularly if one group adheres to liberal Christian values; and prejudice varies as the dominant group oscillates from a mood of guilt and responsibility to one in which the threat to its status is a paramount concern. The stereotypes of the subordinate groups are unmitigated by the patronizing qualities: aggressive, insolent, oversexed, inferior, dangerous and subhuman. The dominant group is often intensely prejudiced and authoritarian, and race relations generally are frequently overtly violent, antagonistic and motivated by hatred.

Here there is no romantic conception of race, but a pattern of beliefs that is intricately related to economic and social situations. Arendt (1958) pertinently observes that although thinking in race categories has its roots in the early eighteenth century, it was not until the emergence of imperialism during the nineteenth century that these views ceased to be eccentric folly and grew to be 'the powerful ideology of imperialistic policies'. What was once a freakish belief, like a conviction that the earth is flat or that flying saucers have landed, became a dangerous justification when the slave trade and 'high capitalism' needed its support.

More specific than Van den Berghe's classification is Simpson and Yinger's analysis in terms of the majority policy towards the minority: (1) assimilation; (2) pluralism; (3) legal protection of minorities; (4) population transfer; (5) continued subjugation; (6) extermination.

1. *Assimilation,* based upon the belief that a stable nation is a homogeneous nation, is illustrated by the modern state of Brazil and (although with gross inconsistencies) by the history of the USA. Cox (1959) describes this as 'the amalgamative situation' and observes that this is an antidote to the emergence of a counter-nationalism by the colonized subordinate groups. though even 'melting-pots' sometimes contain unassimilated lumps, as the American Negroes may prove to be.

2. *Pluralism* is the willingness of the dominant group to permit (or even to encourage) some cultural and social variations within an overall national unity, for example, in modern Soviet policy (except for the opposition to Zionism). In the newly-founded state of Zambia, in which there is a marked and precarious state of cultural and linguistic variation, the government, although firmly in favour of assimilation (the national slogan is 'One Zambia – One Nation'), is becoming compelled to accept the pluralism of some three or more major cultural variations.

3. *Legal protection of minorities* has centred about the controversial principle of national self-determination, which has occasionally

led to such unsatisfactory situations as the struggle between Biafra and Federal Nigeria, and the impossibility of some of the states created by the Treaty of Versailles and the Congress of Berlin lasting as viable units. However, in general terms, such safeguards as the Genocide Convention of the UN, fair employment practices legislation and the protection of civil liberties, will go some way towards ensuring small-group autonomy without hindering the cooperation or organization on a large and feasible scale.

The position in Africa is particularly urgent, as the next generation will probably see the changing of the present (and artificial) national boundaries as 'Balkanization' proves to be increasingly dangerous – economically and politically (see, for example, Nkrumah, 1963, pp. 132–222). It is significant that the Arusha Declaration of the Tanganyika African National Union in January 1967 stressed several times the need for the state to protect minorities against exploitation, and it seems that both cultural and economic exploitation is meant.

4. *Population transfer* is a common measure to prevent assimilation, to reduce tension through physical separation and sometimes to eliminate economic competition. In the last generation, the South African Government has been taking active steps to remove a quarter of a million Africans from their homes in the Western Cape, and the Nazi regime followed the example of Czarist Russia in forced migration of Jews. On the other hand, there is both white and Negro opinion in the USA in favour of solving 'the Negro problem' by a massive return to Africa, and in the nineteenth and early twentieth centuries Negroes did migrate, mostly to the puppet state of Liberia.

5. *Continued subjugation* is the policy of the dominant group that can neither envisage nor afford to drive out the minority nor assimilate them. In South Africa, for example, there is within the ruling National Party a fundamental cleavage developing between the *verligtes* and the *verkramptes*. The former believe in an 'enlightened' form of *apartheid*; the latter believe in the narrowest concepts of domination, based upon fundamentalist Calvinist ideology (see, for example, *Sunday Times*, Johannesburg, 20 August 1967). This is the situation that Cox (1959) describes as

35

'colonial enslavement in which a small aristocracy . . .
exploits large quantities of natural resource, mainly agricultural, with forced . . . labour, raised or purchased like capital
in a slave market, such as that in the pre-Civil War South
and in Jamaica before 1834 – the slavery situation.'

6. *Extermination* is a sickeningly familiar attempt to reduce a
conflict situation, and has a more intricate mixture of irrational
and situational factors than other policies. Within the last
century the Tasmanians have been completely destroyed, and
the American Indians and Hottentots almost completely wiped
out. During the Nazi regime, in barely twelve years, some six
million people were murdered because of their race.

One of the most carefully documented and analysed accounts
of the origins and development of a myth that justified extermination, is the study by Cohn (1970) of the myth that there
is a world-wide Jewish conspiracy to control the world, and
that the forged *Protocols of the Elders of Zion* was the plan of the
organizers of this plot. Despite frequent refutation of the
Protocols, the myth was believed even by quite intelligent people.
Cohn observes that the organizers of massacres or even of anti-
Jewish riots and discrimination varied from 'purely destructive
types' and opportunist, to those who had no alternative that
they could imagine other than to follow a destructive and
violent policy. 'Yet it seems certain that however narrow,
materialistic, or downright criminal their own motives may be,
such men cannot operate without an ideology behind them . . .
to legitimate their behaviour' (Cohn, 1970). A deluded view
of the world is expressed in violent mass behaviour, but the
violence has to be justified by the violent or they cannot escape
the guilt and the shame of seeing themselves as either murderers
and thugs, or accomplices in murder and violence and theft.
A psychoanalyst, Kovel (1970), in his discussion of the psychological history of racism, also emphasizes the manner in which
racism is often integrated into a set of structured beliefs which
provide a framework for the ordering of many of our group
activities. Myths provide meaning, and meanings give ready
reasons for doing things that we would, in other circumstances,
be ashamed or afraid to do.

Race doctrines that have supported these violent attempts to exterminate an alien group have been common during the past century, and it is a melancholy but relevant conclusion to offer a tiny sample.

In 1853 Arthur, Count de Gobineau, published the first of the four volumes of his *Essai sur L'Inégalité des Races Humaines*, which became a prototype for later works on race in history, and was influential as late as World War I as 'one of the chief sources for anti-immigration arguments in the USA' (Gossett, 1965). The *Essai* is intended to demonstrate the superiority of the Aryan race – a race which only existed in Gobineau's imagination and that of his followers. He was interested in discovering the key to human history: why did societies progress at one time and decline at another? What was the single factor responsible for the continuous decline of mankind from heights of excellence 'down towards decrepitude'? With skill, charm and a pessimistic eloquence particularly appealing to those of a paranoiac disposition, Gobineau identified the decline of the French aristocracy with the fall of France, the fall of France with the fall of Western civilization, and the fall of Western civilization with the fall of entire mankind. Had not one small group degenerated, mankind could have been saved. The causes of this degeneration Gobineau attributed to a mixture of races, and he further argued that civilization has always fallen because the superior race – for reasons that are never made clear – failed to keep its 'blood' pure.

Once 'blood mixture' begins, the process is unlikely to be arrested – again for reasons that are unclear – and

'human herds, no longer nations, weighed down by a mournful somnolence, will henceforth be benumbed in their nullity, like buffalo ruminating in the stagnant meres of the Pontine marshes.'

More significant, because of its direct influence upon Alfred Rosenberg, Hitler's theoretician, was Houston Stewart Chamberlain's *The Foundations of the Nineteenth Century*. Chamberlain arranged races in a hierarchy of excellence at the peak of which was the white, particularly the mythical Aryan race. The message of history for Chamberlain was that civilization could only be saved if the struggle between the 'Teutons' and the Jews (and other non-Teutons) was won by the Teutons.

'No arguing about 'humanity' can alter the fact of the struggle. Where the struggle is not waged with cannon-balls, it goes on silently in the heart of society by marriages, by the annhilation of distances which further intercourse.'

Chamberlain was dimly aware of the difficulty of demonstrating any scientific connection between the physical characteristics of race and the behaviour of a specific culture. There is, for example, no more an Aryan culture than there is an Aryan race. He evaded this flaw in his argument by asserting that it is the inner nature of men, not their outward appearance that defines their race, and therefore intuition – *whose* is not clear – proves who is an Aryan and who is not.

World War I stimulated the publication of books and pamphlets on race and race relations, of which Madison Grant's 'The Passing of the Great Race' and Lothrop Stoddard's 'Rising Tide of Colour' were models for even cruder apocalyptic visions of 'superior' races being overwhelmed by 'inferior'.

But the quintessence of this romantic conception of race and the extermination approach to race relations, is Hitler's *Mein Kampf*, on which were based the Third Reich and the New Order in Europe. Hitler claimed that

'all the human culture, all the results of art, science and technology that we see before us today, are almost exclusively the creative product of the Aryan. . . . He is the Prometheus of mankind from whose shining brow the divine spark of genius has sprung at all times.'

Like his predecessors, Hitler believed that 'purity of blood' was essential to maintain the dominant position of the races he claimed to be superior, and he welcomed the corollary that the superior race must struggle and dominate to preserve itself.

'. . . It is no accident that the first cultures arose in places where the Aryan, in his encounters with lower peoples, subjugated them, and bent them to his will. . . . As long as he ruthlessly upheld the master attitude, not only did he remain master, but also the preserver and increaser of culture.'

Such beliefs all too easily provide a spurious justification for the expression of unconscious needs for violence, and it is psychologically no accident that these attitudes led to Auschwitz and Buchenwald and other violent attempts to maintain a mythical superiority and to destroy a fantasy threat.

Chapter 2

HOW RACE AWARENESS GROWS

As long ago as 1890, William James had perceived our dependence upon other people and the groups to which we fancied we belonged, for our appreciation of who we are, and what we are worth in terms of our society.

> '*A man's social self* is the recognition which he gets from his mates. We are not only gregarious animals, liking to be in sight of our fellows, but we have an innate propensity to get ourselves noticed, and noticed favourable, by our kind.
>
> 'Properly speaking, *a man has as many social selves as there are individuals who recognize him* and carry an image of him in their minds. To wound any of these his images is to wound him. But as the individuals who carry the image fall naturally into classes, we may practically say that he has as many different social selves as there are distinct *groups* of persons about whose opinion he cares.' (James, 1890.)

The dilemma of a man who cannot answer the question 'Who am I?' until society has answered the question 'Who is he?' is illuminated by the case of 'T'. In the winter of 1966, two senior judges of the Cape Provincial Division spent two days in attempting to decide who 'T' was – which definition in South Africa depended upon his classification in terms of 'colour'. 'T' had appealed against a decision of the Population Registration Board which had classified him as 'Coloured', and sought to be classified as 'white'.

The Court noted that 'T' received his identity card when he was already twenty-two years old, 'and then became aware for the first time of his classification as a coloured person'. After considerable legal wrangling about the definition of 'white person' in section 1 of the Population Registration Act (30 of 1950), the Court devoted itself to the relevant facts of 'T's' life. Speaking for the Court, Watermeyer, J., observed:

'. . . The Court's first impression was that he was a white man. . . . It is quite obvious that the appellant is not a person who is in appearance obviously not a white person. . . .

'I come now to the facts of the case. The appellant is a young man born on 13 June 1939. His birth certificate indicates that he is a white person. The evidence shows that his father was originally issued with a white identity card but his mother was a coloured woman. The father's origin of his grandmother, or great grandmother, was the Philippines. . . . The appellant grew up . . . mixing, as he says, with both white and coloured children. He was sent to a coloured school. . . . in 1958 the appellant started as a part-time pupil at the University of Cape Town Ballet School . . . and from January 1961, he was employed as a full-time dancer at the school. . . . Appellant says he made a number of white friends at school, but his mother did not wish him to bring them to his home. He subsequently decided to leave home. . . .

'In so far as appellant's private life is concerned, apart from the fact that he occasionally sees his parents and members of the one coloured family I have mentioned, the evidence shows that his present-day associates are all white persons who accept him as a white man.' (T. v. Secretary for the Interior 1966 (3), C.P.D., 565–72).

Until 'T' could answer the question 'Who am I?' he could answer none of the questions that indicate our parameters of living – 'To what can I reasonably aspire? What job or profession can I hope for? Who are my friends? Who are my neighbours? How far in the world can I go?' Had 'T' been confirmed in the status of 'coloured', he would have been confined to a rigidly limited social world in which his status was low and his rights less than those of whites. He would have been placed in the psychologically damaging position of *having to relearn* 'Who am I?' The individual that he had learned to be would suddenly no longer be him. He would have been compelled to live as a different – and inferior – individual.

II. RACIAL IDENTITY IN YOUNG CHILDREN

Social psychologists have been interested since the 1920s in *how* the child comes to be aware of his 'racial' identity and that of other children, and *what consequences* this awareness has for his adult personality.[1]

The Horowitzes (1936, 1939) continued Lasker's pioneer study of 1929 into race attitudes in young children, which was given further impetus by the Clarks (1939). In a series of studies the Horowitzes examined the growth of the attitudes of white boys towards Negroes. They presented to a sample of boys ranging from kindergarten to Grade 8B, photographs of individual white and Negro boys, and photographs of a social situation in which there were either white boys alone or white and coloured boys together. The boys were asked (1) to show their order of preferences from the mixed collection of white and Negro faces and (2) to show which of the boys they would like to bring home to lunch, to play ball with and so on; (3) to show which of the social situations photographed they would like to join.

The degree of prejudice of the boys was estimated by the number of times they accepted members of the white group and the number of time they rejected the Negroes, and it was found that there was not a constant relationship between rejection and acceptance of the Negro at all ages. At the kindergarten level some Negro faces would be preferred and some white, and in some social situations the group with a Negro member would be joined, and in others not. In other words, at an early age the prejudice was highly specific: there was not a general pattern of pro- or anti-Negro attitudes. But as the boys grew older, prejudice on one test was frequently associated with prejudice on the others. A general pattern of prejudice had developed.

[1] Most of the published studies report the growth of awareness of becoming a Negro, but there are studies of white children (Stevenson and Stewart, 1958), Mexicans in Mexico City (Lewis, 1961) and of Maoris in New Zealand (Ausubel, 1961, 1965; Vaughan, 1963), which are strikingly similar to the studies of Negro children. And a series of studies of 'Racism and the French' (Maucorps *et al.*, 1965) is rich in adults' biographical material that often reveals the origins of their awareness of 'race' and their attitudes towards it.

At another stage in their research, the Horowitzes made an intensive study of two small communities in rural Tennessee, where they lived for some months. The question was: *how* does the small child learn the patterns of prejudice that are common to his community?

It was clear that the smallest children were not concerned with race differences, and played with members of any group. Indeed, they had to be taught by more and more severe punishments to leave alone playmates of another race group. One of the most common reasons for spanking children was that they played with those of another race, and it seemed that merely warning them that those of another race were unpleasant or dangerous or disapproved was not enough to change the children's attitudes.

But by the end of primary school, white children had learned the community's race attitudes, and had learned them so thoroughly that their perception and imagination were as indelibly influenced as their emotions. In one test, for example, white children were shown a photograph of a library in which there were only white persons, and were asked 'What was the coloured man doing?' The children always reported that he was dusting the books or sweeping the floor: he was never sitting at a table reading a book. In another test, where a child was asked 'Where do you live?' he answered, 'Fifth house from the station'. The correct answer was seventh from the station, but the child did not count the two houses that belonged to Negroes.

Another example of this selective blindness is from the writer's experience when travelling to Durban. He innocently asked a group of white South African passengers, in conversation, the population of Pietermaritzburg. They gave the small white population correctly, and were quite taken aback when the writer asked for the much larger population of Africans and Indians. Pietermaritzburg was for them a city in which there were only whites.

In the Tennessee study elementary schoolchildren were interviewed by the Horowitzes and among the questions asked were: 'Who tells you what you should do? What kind of children does she tell you not to play with?' The white children said that they were told to play with white children only, and showed an increasing sensitivity to social standards as they were older.

Third and fourth grades (i.e. eight to nine years old) children were already able to reply, 'It looks funny for a white girl to play with a coloured girl' and 'We don't look right playing with her'.

In the first grade a girl would reply 'Momma tells me not to play with black children, keep away from them.' It is clearly an imposed norm, sanctioned by spanking or other punishment, and the Horowitzes suggest that children only gradually, painfully, acquire the race attitudes of their society. At first these attitudes are imposed arbitrarily, then gradually they are introjected and their origins are forgotten, and the child develops the rationalizations that characterize so much adult behaviour.

More recent confirmation of this pattern is described (sometime poignantly) in interviews with white South Africans (Hudson, *et al.*, 1966). The authors are sketching a 'Portrait of a Reactionary':

'The reactionary's experience of the Black man begins at a very early age. In infancy his needs are attended to by a Black nanny. As a boy he is likely to have Black playmates, particularly on a farm, and he may have an older Black servant to look after him as well.

'Let us see what they themselves have to say:

'Children are not conscious of the fact that servants are black and that they themselves are white, and they would kiss the maid, if my wife did not prevent it – when you grow bigger you become more aware of colour – after you first begin to go to school."

'In other quotations . . .

' "We made clay oxen together on the farm and looked after the cattle. When you were little you played together. Later you came to the stage when you became aware it doesn't pay you at all – the lives they lead, the way they dress, and their customs. . . ."

' "After I had gone to school, I became aware that there was a difference – a feeling as of a superior to an inferior came over me." '

The findings of the Horowitzes have often been confirmed and extended, one major series of investigations – that of Kenneth and Mamie Clark – being cited in an influential annex to the appellants' brief to the United States Supreme Court in the 1954 hearings on the desegregation of public schools. The Clarks sought to analyse the origins and development of racial identification, and to relate this identification to the development of the self in Negro children.

In one investigation the Clarks presented children with four dolls that were identical save for their skin colour. Two dolls were brown with black hair and the other two were white with blonde hair. The children were asked the following questions and had to answer by choosing one of the dolls: (1) Give me the doll that you would like to play with – like best; (2) Give me the doll that is a nice doll; (3) Give me the doll that looks bad. (4) Give me the doll that is a nice colour; (5) Give me the doll that looks like a white child; (6) Give me the doll that looks like a coloured child; (7) Give me the doll that looks like a Negro child; (8) Give me the doll that looks like you.' (Clark & Clark, 1958.) The requests 1–4 were to reveal the child's preferences; 5–7 to show if the child recognized 'racial differences'; and 8 to show self-identification.

Two hundred and fifty-three Negro children took part in the study, of whom more than half were tested in segregated nursery schools and state schools, and who had had no experience of a racially integrated school. The other group were tested in racially integrated schools in Massachusetts. The ages of the children ranged from three to seven, rather more than half were female, in skin colour half were medium-light, slightly less than a third were dark and slightly less than a fifth were light (i.e. 'practically white').

Possibly the most striking observations were the emotional reactions of some of the children towards the test, and it should be borne in mind that the Clarks are themselves Negroes:

'. . . Some of the children who were free and relaxed in the beginning of the experiment broke down and cried or became somewhat negativistic during the latter part when they were required to make self-identifications. . . . This type of behaviour, although not so extreme, was more prevalent in the North than in the South.'

On the whole the children rejected the black and preferred the white dolls for simple and direct reasons: 'cause he's white' or 'cause he's pretty', for the white doll. The brown doll was often described as ugly or rejected 'cause him black' or 'got black on him'.

The Clarks found that their data 'definitely indicate that a basic knowledge of "racial differences" exists as a part of the pattern of ideas of Negro children from the age of three through seven years on the northern and southern communities tested . . . and that this knowledge develops more definitely from year to year to the point of absolute stability at the age of seven.' Furthermore, the children used the term 'Negro' as a verbalization of these differences, and the Clarks suggest that attendance at public schools encouraged the use of this term.

The children's identification of the dolls by skin colour varied with the children's own skin colour. The darker children seemed more definite in their knowledge of racial differences, and the medium and dark children *as a group* were more sensitive than were the light children.

The study also showed that the majority of these children preferred the white doll and rejected the coloured doll. About two-thirds showed that they liked the white doll 'best', or that they would prefer to play with the white doll, and that the white doll was 'nice doll'. Correspondingly, they showed negative or hostile attitudes towards the brown doll.

A comparison of the northern and southern children revealed no significant differences. Both groups knew well which doll was white and which was brown, but the northern made fewer identifications with the coloured doll and more with the white, which might reflect the higher proportion of light children in the North and less intense concern with colour difference.

Finally, the Clarks found rationalizations among both northern and southern children for their rejection of the brown doll, for example 'he looks bad 'cause he hasn't got an eyelash'. And one five-year-old explained his identification with the brown doll by stating 'I burned my face and made it spoil.'

More recent confirmation of the Clarks' findings has come from psychiatry, for example in Adam (1950) and Brody (1963).

Brody made a study of colour and identity conflict in young

boys in urban Baltimore, and concluded from his psychiatric appraisal that

'. . . many of these Negro boys do have significant conflicts involving anxiety or guilt-laden wishes to be white rather than Negro. In this sense some may be considered uncertain as to their identities. Some seem to have little ambivalence or uncertainty, and clearly noted their wish to be white and their repressed feelings about being dark-skinned.'

Even at the age of four Brody's patients were not only able to perceive themselves as black and, therefore, not the same as other white children, but were showing some symptoms of emotional disturbance that derived from unsatisfactory answers that society offered to the question, 'Who am I?'

Brody had the boys play with glove puppets, one white and the other brown, and observed their attitudes towards them. For example, E. B. aged five was handling the white puppet, and Brody's case-notes read:

'Resembles self and father, is bad. Negro fights, is bad. People call him "black stuff" and he doesn't like it. "I would rather be called brown than black. I like white people. I don't like brown people. I don't like myself." '

And K. H. aged six, playing with the white puppet:

'Resembles brother. Friendly puppet interaction, but White puppet is drunk, hit on head "by light-skinned person", has more money, is happy, might "knock Negro out", while Negro is sad. At first says he likes White best, that White resembles him but finally: "Negro is more like me . . . I'm dark-skinned . . . light skin is the best . . . light is prettier . . . light skin is too light . . . I never wanted to have a light skin." '

A sophisticated and sensitive study has been made of the 'difference in the personality structure and development of Maori and pakeha adolescents . . .' (pakeha = European, 'white'). The practical questions from which the study developed were those of keeping Maori youth in school beyond fifteen and of increasing Maori participation in skilled trades and in the professions. The Maori youth face discrimination, economically and socially, and have little encouragement from their parents to progress educationally and vocationally. Ausubel implies that the pattern of discrimination and lack of positive encouragement tend to make the Maori youth feel that he is a different person from his pakeha coevals.

The Maori peer-group in the early adolescent and adolescent years is more cohesive and more protective to its members than that of pakehas, and this seems to be a result of the persisting prejudice by pakehas against the Maoris.

It was observed that

> 'Maori boys are either sullen, defiant, and unruly in school or else adopt a completely apathetic attitude. Racial pride among these pupils has a somewhat chauvinistic and anti-pakeha flavour. They make little effort to better themselves, to reflect credit on their ethnic group, or to acquire a working knowledge of the Maori language or a genuine understanding of Maori culture, but are just fiercely and militantly proud of being maoris and not pakehas.' (Ausubel, 1956.)

Yet, like American Negro adolescents (and even those in Africa from areas relatively little touched by 'Western' adolescent culture),[1] Maori adolescents wear the gear, talk the slang, display the symptoms of maladjustment of their white coevals, and, no doubt, are correspondingly groping for a self-identification – not exclusively as Maoris but as teenagers like other teenagers.

III. AWARENESS OF SELF

The development of self-awareness is mediated to the child by the attitudes of his or her family. The family does not need to make specific pronouncements about the social meaning of the child's colour or 'race'. Approval and disapproval can be communicated by implicit acceptance and rejection of attitudes

---

[1] For example, recently in Zambia, the writer was charmed and astonished to meet in a bar two Africans aged about twenty, dressed as their fellows in London: flower-patterned shirts and ties, tight striped pants with broad belts, and pale blue linen Beatle caps perched on top of stretched teased hair. And this in a country where such smart, imported clothes are difficult to obtain and are expensive.

and behaviour. The child learns *how* to be a Negro or a white or a Maori; he is aware that he is one and can articulate his belongingness. He acquires a picture about the worth (or worthlessness) of his social and his bodily self from his earliest contacts with other members of his family, his peers, his teachers, what he sees on the movies, TV, advertisements, in what he reads, in the conversations he overhears, and from the daily observation of who sits next to him, who moves away from him, who appears to want him.

Psychoanalysts have been reluctant to discuss the effects of 'race' upon ego development, but L. S. Kubie (1965) has made a provocative analysis of the development of racial prejudice. He relates prejudice to three factors in childhood: (1) The prejudiced child's attitudes toward his body are ambivalent: mingled shame and a guilty, secretive pride. He both loves his body and has a strong aversion to it. (2) He is unable to conceive that one day he will be an adult. He cannot face the future without fear, and he wishes for ever to remain the child who is dependent and who nevertheless can paradoxically manipulate the world to satisfy his wishes. (3) He is unable to accept the anatomical differences between the sexes. His own sexual attitudes are compounded of 'feminine dependence' and 'masculine dominance', and a tough, outward masculinity conceals a wish for passive 'feminine', homosexual dependence.

A source of information that is becoming increasingly valuable is the psychological novel. The early psychological novel of, say, Proust and James were almost entirely confined to the meticulous exploration of the alchemy of the relationship of one individual to another, and were only peripherally concerned with the psychological disturbances brought about by the social clashes of class, race or culture. Richard Wright, James Baldwin and many other authors, who belong to minority groups, have added a new dimension. The modern psychological novel is primarily concerned with group involvements, and an individual may be portrayed as a representative of his group rather than as an autonomous individual. The older introspective privacy has been banished by the clash of society.

In a study with a social-psychological approach, White

D

49

(1947) made a value-analysis of the autobiography of the Negro author Richard Wright – *Black Boy*. The book and White's analysis give a convincing portrait of a 'tragically unhappy' early life. But it is not easy to tell from the book or the analysis the extent to which the unhappiness was due to Wright's race in a hostile white world, and to what extent some of his experiences might be found in any frustrated family struggling to maintain its integrity despite poverty, uncertainty and low status.

White counted 1,205 instances of frustration, but only 349 instances of satisfaction – hunger was frequent, 'many biscuits piled high upon the bread platter' were rare. Anger, hostility, aggression, disapproval of other people were very frequent: 'I stood fighting, fighting as I had never fought in my life, fighting with myself . . . and I was trying to stifle the impulse to go the drawer of the kitchen table and get a knife and defend myself . . .'; 'watching the white people eat would make my empty stomach churn, and I would grow vaguely angry'; 'we threw rocks (at the white boys who came on our side of the boundary-line), cinders, coal, sticks, pieces of iron, and broken bottles, and while we threw them we longed for even deadlier weapons.'

By far the greatest number of hostile references are to Southern whites, followed far behind by members of the family, and involve incidents in which Richard is handled violently for some real – or fancied – infringement of Southern race etiquette.

Wright asks himself time and again: 'What was it that made the hate of whites for blacks so steady, so seemingly woven into the texture of things?' and hates himself for his impotence, that is sharpened by his awareness:

'I could not believe in my feelings. My personality was numb, reduced to a lumpish, loose, dissolved state. I was a non-man, something that knew vaguely that it was human but felt that it was not. . . . My words were innocent, but they indicated, it seemed, a consciousness on my part that infuriated white people. . . .

'I had begun coping with the white world too late. I could not make subservience an automatic part of my behaviour.

I had to feel and think out each tiny item of racial experience
. . . and to each item I brought the whole of my life.'

By the time that Richard Wright was a young adolescent
'with almost seventeen years of baffled living behind him', he
trusted no one, loved no one. He had lived in an atmosphere of
violence, alone and isolated from both Negroes and whites. As
he puts it '. . . my life at home had cut me off, not only from
white people but from Negroes as well', but this family life was
one that could not be understood apart from the social context
of the South in which it was embodied, the shattered life of a
bright boy in a shattered family broken by the pressures of a
hostile society.

On the last page of *Black Boy*, Richard Wright leaves the
South where he was raised and heads north, not towards a
millennium but to escape into reality. He went

'to fling myself into the unknown . . . I fled so that the numb-
ness of my defensive living might thaw out and let me feel
the pain – years later and far away – of what living in the
South had meant.'

Many other authors who are Negroes, or members of a
minority group that suffers some discrimination, have described
their youth in similar terms. As long ago as in the 1890s Israel
Zangwill wrote the classic (and underestimated) *Children of the
Ghetto* about the life of recent Jewish immigrants to the East
End of London, and later a wealth of Yiddish novels and
poetry appeared by, *inter alia*, Scholem Asch and Isaac Singer.

The isolation and uncertainty of growing up to be a Negro
is one example of growth within any minority group, but three
writers are peculiarly worth noting because of the clarity of
their insight: James Baldwin, Ralph Ellison and Malcolm X.

The crucial thread running through these three writers'
work is that a normally secure and status-satisfying life is
impossible for the Negro in the USA. The Negro can never
answer the question 'Who am I?' truthfully and with satisfaction and pride, because the definition of the role of the Negro
given to him by white society is one of low status and rejection.
And throughout Baldwin, Ellison and Malcolm X, Negroes
are portrayed as fighting the role of subordinates – sometimes

defeated, sometimes victorious. Membership of a minority group compels the Negro to hate himself and his Negro-ness as much as he may hate the whites. The child who grows up a Negro knows that he has a society ranged against him.

In the form of a 'Letter to my nephew', Baldwin observes with fierce starkness:

> 'You were born where you were born and faced the future that you faced because you were black and *for no other* reason. The limits of your ambition were, thus, expected to be set forever. You were born into society which spelled out with brutal clarity . . . that you were a worthless human being. You were not expected to aspire to excellence: you were expected to make peace with mediocrity.' (Baldwin, 1963.)

Particularly significant in Baldwin's work is the frequency with which a Negro is compelled to acknowledge his inferior status, and to respond destructively and hopelessly, either harming himself or hurting those who wish to be his friends. Baldwin infuses his portraits of the Negro with a strong taint of paranoia.

One example: before he commits suicide, Rufus in *Another Country* says to his friend Vivaldo, who is white,

> 'How I hate them all those white sons of bitches out there. They got the world on a string . . . and they tying that string around my neck, they killing me . . . I want to hear them *crying*, man, for somebody to come and help them. . . . I think wouldn't it be nice to get on a boat and go some place . . . where a man could be treated like a man. . . . You got to fight with the landlord because the landlord's white. . . .'

The Negro inhabits 'another country' and in his own and that of the whites nobody knows his name. The hostile anonymity thrust upon him from his early childhood saps his self-reliance, wilts his intelligence and shrivels his spontaneity.

More immediately factual than Baldwin's (apparently) autobiographical novel is *The Autobiography of Malcolm X* (Haley and Malcolm X, 1966). Again the violence, the poverty and the fragmented family. Again the young boy discouraged by the burden of being born a Negro.

To a psychologist the most significant theme throughout the statements of Malcolm X is the destructive effect of discrimination upon the identity of the Negro, and upon the white man himself: 'the American white man's malignant superiority complex', that is built upon his 'pattern, this "system" . . . of teaching Negroes to hide the truth from him behind a façade of grinning, "yessir-bossing", foot shuffling and head-scratching.'

Further: 'the black man in North America was mentally sick in his cooperative, sheeplike acceptance of the white man's culture.' A similar theme is found in the speeches of politicians of independent Africa, for instance, the Minister of Foreign Affairs of Zambia, then Mr Simon Kapepwe, is reported as saying that 'a nation that constantly aped the culture of another nation was a dead one, even though it was politically independent'. In the same report he said that 'the worst thing colonization had done in Africa was to indoctrinate African minds, leaving them to think that the only right practice was that done by a European. . . .'

The psychological evidence for and against this assertion will be examined in a later chapter.

Malcolm X, like Baldwin's characters, sought during youth for an identity, for a group to which to belong was satisfying and meaningful. Baldwin's characters never find such belonging, save by a retreat from society into an intimate relationship of one person with another, usually of a homosexual kind. Malcolm X found nothing until he became a member of 'The Brotherhood', and at last felt that he, hitherto just one more of America's Negroes, was part of a world-wide community. After his *hajj* to Mecca, he made a speech in which he stated, 'I *know* once and for all that the Black Africans look upon America's 22 million blacks as long-lost *brothers*! They *love* us! . . . They were so *happy* to hear how we are awakening from our long sleep. . . .'

Whatever be the factual basis for Malcolm X's assertion, there seems to be little doubt that some American Negroes have begun to regard the African society as a reference group.

But the most imaginative treatment of the Negro awareness is probably Ralph Ellison's novel *Invisible Man* – a curious amalgam: as bizarre as *Candide* and as intense as *Moby Dick*. Again the theme is the estrangement and isolation of the young Negro and his struggle to discover who he is. The difference is that Ellison does not portray realistic characters in realistic situations, but alludes to the situation of the American Negro in a series of near-fantastic incidents.

The key passage is that which opens the book:

'I am an invisible man. No, I am not a spook like those who haunted Edgar Allan Poe; nor am I one of your Hollywood movie ectoplasms. I am a man of substance, of flesh and bone, fibre and liquids – and I might even be said to possess a mind. I am invisible, understand, simply because people refuse to see me. . . .

'That invisibility to which I refer occurs because of a peculiar disposition of the eyes of those with whom I come into contact. A matter of the construction of their *inner* eyes, those eyes with which they look through their physical eyes upon reality.'

IV. CONCEPTUALIZING GROUP DIFFERENCES

A white friend of the writer was recently driving with his daughter aged four and a half through the slum area of Kalingalinga, a few miles from Lusaka. 'Why do Africans have to live in horrible, dirty houses?' 'Not all Africans have to live in horrible, dirty houses.' 'Yes. But *why* is it *they* have to live in horrible, dirty houses?' 'Because most Africans are poor, and can't afford nice big houses.' 'Why is it that people the same colour as us live in nice, big houses?' 'Well, our house is given to us by the government.' 'Why doesn't the government build nice houses for the poor Africans?' 'Because there isn't enough money.' 'But if they've got enough money to build nice houses for people like us, why can't they build houses for the poor Africans too?'

A few days later the conversation was resumed in slightly different terms. We were driving along a pleasant, residential area: 'Why is it that in Jubilee Road there are nice houses and *all* the Africans live in nasty houses?' 'But not all Africans live in nasty houses. You know where Uncle Saul lives?' After a long pause: 'His wife isn't an African is she?'

In fact both Saul Mwanza and his wife are Africans, but the child found it difficult to perceive them as Africans. She had already associated poverty with being an African, and

being white was associated with wealth. She had already cate-
gorized Africans with poverty, though without any feeling of
hostility or distance, and this categorization had been formed
despite her attending a school in which there were African
children. She had African friends, and her parents had African
friends and visitors.

Mary Goodman (1964) for example studied 103 four-year-
olds, both white and coloured, living in a city in the north-
eastern part of the USA. Goodman found that these small
children not only recognized themselves as light or dark-skinned,
but classified groups in much the same way as adults. Thomas,
for example,

> 'looked thoughtfully at the children in his room at school
> and said: "There are two white children here and all the
> rest are coloured." Any adult would have said the same, and
> the "coloured" ranged from very light to medium dark.'

She found that the children were keenly concerned with
variations in skin colour and in hair form, and spent much time
stroking or feeling each other's hair. But most significantly the
children associated ways of life with colour differences, even
when they were themselves not acutely aware of, or sensitive to,
differences of colour. Joan 'told us: "The people that are white
they can go up. The people that are brown, they have to go
down." '

Accompanying these generalized concepts about the relative
status of Whites and Negroes, the Children displayed strong
attitudes of rejection or acceptance of their colour. One of the
boys liked only white dolls and white people in pictures he was
shown and rejected brown dolls and people violently: 'He's
black! He's stinky little boy – He's a stinker – he sh—!' . . .
He added: 'I don't like coloured boys.' Sometimes the children
even denied their colour: 'Sam (N) playing "fireman" with
Ian (W) and Nathan (W). Sam observed casually, "There are
two white firemen". John (N and quite dark) asserts: "I'm the
white boy," upon hearing another child murmurs something
about a "black girl". James (N and quite light) corrects John:
"No – you're a dark boy". No reply from John.'

Goodman concluded that 'it is all too clear that Negro
children not yet five can sense that they are marked, and grow

uneasy. They can like enormously what they see across the colour line, and find it hard to like what they see on their side. In this there is scant comfort or security, and in it are the dynamics for rending personality asunder.'

Fanon (1970) has explored the personality consequences of 'The white man sealed in his whiteness. The black man in his blackness' as a psychiatrist seeking to enhance the healthy components of a pathological situation, with the aim of increasing the former where the pathology could not be cured. There is increasing evidence that black identity is no longer overwhelmingly composed of pathological elements in which the extent to which the individual could not compare favourably with whites made him feel inadequate or inferior. The black man is growing proud of being sealed in his blackness, and indifferent to the white man who is sealed in his whiteness. Blackness and whiteness are seen as distinct and blackness is no matter for shame or guilt, because blacks are everywhere seen as asserting themselves politically and socially. Erikson (1968) has analysed the problem of 'Race and the Wider Identity' and was encouraged by the emergence of blacks as individuals in their own right, rather than as mosaics of negatives. He sees the 'widespread preoccupation with identity . . . not only as a symptom of "alienation" but also as a corrective trend in historical evolution . . . what is at stake here is nothing less than the realization of the fact and the obligation of man's specieshood'; and the corollary is the dwindling of the emphasis upon a psychological and politically limited pseudospecies of 'blackness' in stark opposition to 'whiteness'. Both are becoming subsumed under 'humanness'.

Children identify themselves also in terms of membership of a national group, and here too they construct general categories of preferences and stereotypes.

Piaget (1928) studied the development of judgement and reasoning of boys between seven and ten in Geneva, and found they could with difficulty think and handle such apparently simple ideas as that of kinship, country, town or district. This he argued was because of their inability to relate the part to the whole. For example, 'up to the age of nine, three-quarters of the children denied the possibility of being both Swiss and Genevan (or Vaudois, etc.). . . . Is it perhaps due to local patriotism? We never discovered any trace of it. . . . It is simply [an idea] that had never occurred to them. Often it even struck them as eccentric.'

Piaget concluded that the inability to distinguish part from whole was an aspect of the child's egocentric 'habit of sticking to the immediate point of view . . . a complete lack of relativity, or what comes to the same thing, a complete inability to handle the logic of relations'.

Similarly, the race-awareness and race-identification of children seem equally to display an inability to differentiate *within and across* the groupings into Negro and white. The causes of this inability are probably to be found deeply embedded in our culture and methods of formal education.

Gustav Jahoda's studies of Scottish children's ideas of nationality and attitudes about other countries confirms much of Piaget's earlier work.[1] He distinguished three very general age levels: 6–7, 8–9 and 10–11, which he summarizes:

'rudimentary concepts of home country; fails to understand "foreign"; can name few if any other countries; no coherent space-time orientation.

'concept of home country established; understands "foreign" and can name several other countries; partial space-time orientation emerging.

'geographical and historical concepts in the stricter sense are beginning to be mastered; political and economic ideas make their appearance.' (Jahoda, G., 1962.)

He observes that strangeness and foreignness are associated with language differences and appearance, but that this is not always spontaneously associated with prejudice. He also makes the interesting observation that contemporary events influenced the children's attitudes and ideas:

'many even of the youngest ones had heard about the Russian sputnik. . . . Their image of Russia as austere, but techno-

---

[1] Other studies include: Tajfel, H. 'Children and foreigners', *New Society*, 30 June, 1966; Tajfel H. and Jahoda, G. 'Development in children of concepts and attitudes about their own and other nations: a cross-national study', *Proceedings of the XVIIth International Congress of Psychology*, Moscow 1966, Symposium 36, pages 17–33.

logically advanced, favourably contrasted with the chromium plate and candy-floss picture of America ("their biggest thing is films").'

Allport holds that 'prejudice was not *taught* by the parent but was *caught* from an infected atmosphere' (Allport, 1954), and probably the child's awareness of who he is, and what this means in terms of his life, is 'caught' rather than 'taught'. But it is still necessary to understand *who* catches and *who* resists catching prejudice and an unhealthy race-awareness. The next chapter discusses these problems, taking as a starting-point investigations of authoritarianism as a personality characteristic.

Chapter 3

PERSONALITY AND
RACIAL ATTITUDES

I. INTRODUCTION

How far are our racial attitudes determined by our early experiences in the family? The psychoanalysts have made much of this influence and a social psychologist must make an assessment of the influence of early life.

Ethnocentricism is an exaggerated tendency to rate one's own race (or national or tribal group) as superior to other groups. It is associated with a rigid insistence that the standards of one's own group should be the standards for all groups, and usually includes an acute sensitivity to race (or national or tribal) membership. It is the social equivalent of individual morbid conceit, and when it hardens into chauvinism it is as disruptive as an individual whose life is dominated by megalomania.

Ethnocentricism is not necessarily associated with overt hostility towards members of groups perceived as alien. Indeed the example of proselytizing missionaries shows that it can be effectively masked by a superficially benevolent interest in other groups. But often the group that is perceived as inferior is also perceived as a threat, and this leads to a reluctance to permit informal and intimate contact with it, and to the erection of social, legal or political barriers.

Like all attitudes ethnocentricism is neither exclusively social nor individual in its origins. Sometimes it is a widely accepted and normal part of society's pattern of values, as among South African whites or in many colonial and ex-colonial societies. Or, it might originate in the peculiarities of an individual's upbringing. But most often social and individual factors are jointly responsible. A person without psychopathological hatred, distrust or sensitivity may hold ethnocentric attitudes because they are the social norms that he has learned. A person who does have deep needs to hate and distrust may divert these towards values other than ethnocentric, if his society provides him with few or no ethnocentric norms or disapproves of them. But he may reveal his latent ethnocentricism in a society that encourages or permits expression of these individual needs.

Even the most stringently sociological approach, however, would concede to the parents a role more than mediators or transmitters of culture. It is in the matrix of the family in the child's most dependent years that his basic attitudes and social awareness are formed. In particular, his attitudes towards others and to himself on which are based his social, political and religious attitudes and sympathies are indelibly coloured by his first few years of learning what people are like.

II. THE FAMILY AND RACE ATTITUDES

Race attitudes and race awareness are communicated by the parents in the same way that they communicate to the child the social significance of their class membership or political affiliations. Moreover, the nature and quality of *what* the parents transmit depends upon the subtle interplay between parents and child. The attitudes and awareness may be transmitted accurately or there may be some idiosyncratic distortion or adaptation. The parents may communicate them in such an implicitly critical or reluctant way that the result is to teach the reverse of what society defines. For example, Kardiner & Oversey (1965) report cases in which Negro children have been punished severely by their mothers when they have infringed the norms of deferential behaviour by Negroes towards whites, but for the child's protection and without the mother disguising her own hatred of whites and the standard set by white society for Negroes.

Much of the research on the development of sensitivity towards race attempts to relate the personality characteristics of the parents to the attitudes they communicated to their children, and is influenced by psychoanalytical views of child development.

A major stimulus to later research has been that of Else

Frenkel-Brunswik (1948) which was designed 'to throw light on the determinants of susceptibility to racial or ethnic prejudice . . . in children', and found that even eleven-year-old children had fairly consistent attitudes, which seemed to be related to personality characteristics. The prejudiced child and the un-prejudiced child displayed differing personality features, and their prejudices formed a part of a broader pattern of attitudes towards men and society.

The study was of children from eleven to sixteen, totalling 1,500 boys and girls of varying socio-economic backgrounds who were studied by means of psychological tests and interviews. Parents of the children were also interviewed. Of these children 120 were found to be extremely prejudiced or unprejudiced, and they and their parents were specially interviewed.

The study revealed a remarkably typical pattern of contrasts between the prejudiced and unprejudiced children, from the following characteristics:

1. General social attitudes
2. Attitudes towards weakness
3. Attitudes towards power and money
4. Attitudes of submission to parents and teachers
5. Attitudes towards morality and conformity
6. Intolerance of ambiguities
7. Conception of the world as dangerous or safe

1. The ethnocentric children were more concerned with matters that related to their immediate welfare and comfort, and were unable to think in terms of 'far-reaching social good'. The ethnocentric children rejected the out-group and accepted the in-group naïvely and selfishly. The ethnocentric children, for example, supported statements such as 'if we keep having labour troubles, we may have to turn the government over to a dictator who will prevent any more strikes' and 'only people who are like myself have a right to be happy'. On the other hand, the tolerant children listed as problems 'the atom bomb; how to do things about the atom bomb to keep peace in the world'.

2. 'The aggression of the ethnocentric children is not limited to minority groups and other countries but is a part of a much more generalized rejection of all that is weak or different.'

The prejudiced child agreed that 'the world would be perfect if we put on a desert island all the weak, crooked and feeble-minded people', and disagreed that 'it is interesting to be friends with someone who thinks or feels differently from the way you do'.

Ethnocentric children tend also to equate masculinity with strength and femininity with weakness, and rigidly to distinguish the roles of the sexes. The ethnocentric child rejects equalitarianism between the sexes, and is less likely to make an adequate heterosexual adjustment than the liberal child.

3. 'The contempt the ethnocentric child has for the weak is related to his admiration of the strong, tough, and powerful, *per se.*' He often agrees that 'might makes right; the strong win out in the end', and his fear of weakness is expressed in his agreeing that 'if a person does not watch out somebody will make a sucker out of him'. Similarly, prejudiced children see money as a means to obtain power, material things and even friends: 'No dollar, no friend; have a dollar, got a friend.' Correspondingly, they exaggerate the evil of money as much as its importance.

4. The ethnocentric child *needs* to submit to authority, to strict discipline and punishment: 'It would be better if teachers would be more strict', and the perfect father is described as one who 'does not give you everything you want . . . doesn't let you do the outrageous things that you sometimes want to do'. He is a negative parent, restrictive rather than accepting. Frenkel-Brunswik comments that these children both submitted to authority, but were fearful of it, but that the unprejudiced children do not long for strong authority, nor do they need to assert the importance of strength.

Yet the ethnocentric child is not one who feels free to express his aggression. His concern with authority and hierarchy is repressive, and their hostility has often to be concealed. Hence the ethnocentric child's 'explosive' aggression and the appeal of socially-approved aggression such as war and fascism. The liberal child may be aggressive, but this is milder and is less destructive to his personality equilibrium.

All children, tolerant or intolerant, are aggressive, and all have to learn the forbidden and the permitted modes of satisfying their aggression. But in some societies aggression is supported or encouraged, in others it is discouraged, and in yet others it may be deflected to relatively benevolent ends even if it cannot be harmlessly dissipated.

It is a weakness of the argument of *The Authoritarian Personality* that it treats aggression as though it were an emotional constant that can be neither manipulated nor reduced by a social system or by the narrow family. But the twentieth century is so dangerous not because there is a larger reservoir of aggression about to burst the dams, but because society does so much to permit or to foster the expression of overt hostility and aggression. This is a world in which it is difficult for the child to grow up tolerant.

5. The ethnocentric child is a conforming child: he approves the external forms of morality, and is conventional. He has a punitive super-ego, and has a greater tendency towards moralistic condemnation. His mind is 'closed' rather than 'open'. His judgements are inflexible. His morality is fearful.

6. The ethnocentric child's inflexibility is associated with his reluctance to tolerate situations in which there is doubt and the possibility of choice. Even where there need be no social or emotional involvement, for example, in solving arithmetical problems, he resists changing his way of tackling the problem once he has made up his mind. A simple solution and a rigid approach reduces the area of uncertainty and the anxieties that uncertainty generates.[1] The liberal child does not seek to deny his weakness nor is he as threatened by anxiety.

7. The ethnocentric child sees the world as a place full of danger, chaos, and the possibility of catastrophe. He feels helplessly exposed and often accepts bizarre and superstitious beliefs.

Frenkel-Brunswik's conclusions are moderate and with practical implications: 'from the point of view of society as a whole, the most important problem therefore seems to be the child's attitude towards authority. Forced submission to authority produces only surface conformity countermanded by violent underlying destructiveness, dangerous to the very society to which there seems to be conformity.'

A careful study by Mussen and Naylor (1954), using a combination of observed-behaviour and a standard personality

[1] See Rokeach, M., *The Open and Closed Mind*, New York. Basic Books, 1960.

test, supports much of Frenkel-Brunswik's position. They investigated twenty boys, mostly white, aged from 9–10 to 15–18, who had been referred to the Bureau of Juvenile Research in Columbus, Ohio, for behaviour problems, such as stealing, truancy, etc.

They found strong support for the view that those boys with a great amount of aggressive fantasy indulged in more overt aggression than the boys with little aggressive fantasy. Boys with 'a high ratio of anticipation of punishment to aggressive needs' showed little overt aggression, though their aggressive needs were still there. In other words, outward conformity can mask inner turbulence, and it is not unreasonable to infer that a change in the external conditions may permit (or even encourage) the formerly repressed aggression to be expressed in disruptive behaviour.

Mosher and Scodel (1960) further explored the relationship between 'ethnocentrism in children and the ethnocentrism and authoritarian rearing practices of their mothers', and suggested a modification of Frenkel-Brunswik's position.

They administered a test of ethnocentrism to 400 children in grades 6 and 7 in a middle-class suburb of Columbus, Ohio, and to their mothers they sent a questionnaire designed both to measure ethnocentrism and authoritarian child-rearing practices. They then compared scores of parent and child.

The results 'unequivocally support the conclusion that ethnic attitudes of children are related to the ethnic attitudes of their mothers'. The mothers who scored high on ethnocentrism tended to have children who similarly scored high, and those mothers who scored low had children who scored low. But the results 'cast doubts on the existence of any significant relationship between ethnic attitudes of children and the authoritarian rearing practices of their mothers'.

They explain this in terms of the specific nature of learning of attitudes. It is relatively straightforward to pick up the mother's ethnocentric attitudes. It is less simple to trace a connection between the mother's authoritarian child-rearing practices and specific behaviour by the child. Authoritarianism is a personality characteristic and only gradually and cumulatively becomes crystallized in the child's reactions to his life-experience. Further, the resentment and frustration that authoritarian rearing might create can find many outlets, which need not include the development of hostile attitudes towards minority groups. An acute conflict can arise in which the authoritarian rearing contrasts with moderate or liberal social and political attitudes. This is the case of the aggressive pacifist (Glover, 1947), who defends his political pacifism with a ferocious emotional involvement, and often with authoritarian methods.[1]

III. THE AUTHORITARIAN ADULT

In May 1944 'The Authoritarian Personality' project was launched, at a time when the gravest political issue was the struggle between fascism and opposing ideologies. The earliest emphasis was, therefore, on the personality dynamics of adherence to fascist ideology, and only later was the concept of authoritarianism applied to such areas as art, science, literature, philosophy and education, where fascism and ethnocentricism may be latent rather than manifest. It also became recognized that not only conservatives and 'reactionaries' are authoritarian, but radicals, liberals and the non-political may also show an authoritarian personality structure.

The authors found that they could differentiate various types of extremely high and extremely low authoritarianism, among which are the 'conventional' and the 'authoritarian' (among the high scorers) and the 'easy-going' and the 'genuine liberal' (among the low scorers).

The *conventional* is an individual who accepts stereotypes and generalizations that his society offers him and closely integrates them into his personality. Among this type is 'the well-bred anti-Semite', whose prejudiced beliefs and attitudes do not permit the expression of overt violence or hostility, and whose prejudice centres about pseudo-intellectual arguments for the separation of 'in' and 'out' groups. Many of the more sincere apologists for *apartheid* in South Africa are of this type. The model type is the *authoritarian*. He needs to submit to authority

---

[1] See Eysenck, H. J., *The Psychology of Politics* (Routledge, 1964); and 'Primary, social attitudes: A comparison of attitude patterns in England, Germany and Sweden' (*Journal of Abnormal and Social Psychology*, 1953, **48**, 563–8); and Flugel, J. C., *Man, Morals and Society*, Peregrine Books, 1965.

and yet subconsciously rebels against authority and resents it. His repressed resentment against authority is deflected to a hatred of out-groups that is often openly violent. Anxious, angry, punitive, lacking insight, he seems to be driven by his barely controlled and deeply unsettled emotions. Fearing his own open violence, yet needing to express it, he perceives the world as filled with groups whose behaviour threatens him and his race or nation, and therefore justify his violence. Violence thus becomes counter-violence, and some part of its component of guilt is neutralized. Even the lynching-party needs to satisfy itself that it is performing a socially valuable service.

In sharp contrast are the 'easy-going' and the 'genuine liberal'. The *easy-going* individual is imaginative, and has a sense of humour and capacity for enjoyment. He is unwilling to commit himself or to do violence. His attitude is one of 'live and let live'. He lacks anxiety and has little sense of acquisitiveness, because of his secure childhood and his pleasant relations with his mother. The *genuine liberal*, unlike the easy-going, is very outspoken and has firm opinions about social and political issues. He is close to reality and does not think in stereotypes, and his identifying with those whom he thinks are repressed does not blind him to the dangers of a compensatory over-concern. He values independence, and while valuing and defending his own beliefs he will not interfere with those of other people.

Significantly, the high and the low scorers gave contrasting accounts of their childhoods. The high scorers tended to describe an idealized and stereotyped picture at the beginning of the interview, and when they were closely questioned they allowed critical features to creep in. The low scorers tried to be objective throughout the interview, mentioning both the good and the bad features of their parents.

Frenkel-Brunswik (1954) summarizes the contrasting families:

'. . . warmer, closer and more affectionate interpersonal relationships prevail in the homes of the unprejudiced children. . . . In the home with the orientation toward rigid conformity, on the other hand, actual maintenance of discipline is often based upon the expectation of a quick learning of external, rigid and superficial rules which are bound to be beyond the comprehension of the child. Family relationships are characterized by fearful subservience to the demands of the parents and by an early suppression of impulses not acceptable to the adults.'

The approach of *The Authoritarian Personality* has been highly influential in guiding the pattern of more recent research about political affiliation and belief. Its value is that it indicates some of the personality variables that determine susceptibility to prejudice and ethnocentricism – or that encourage resistance to such beliefs. According to this approach, oversensitivity to race (or another socially defined in-group) is an integral part of the individual's fundamental personality and his perception of the world, and is only indirectly responsive to social norms. It appears to follow that any wide-scale attempt to alleviate racism must begin within the family and the earlier school-days when personality characteristics are still being formed.

This view, seductively simple, would probably no longer be held by the authors of *The Authoritarian Personality* as tenaciously as in the 1940s, because it becomes increasingly well established that *most* individuals with prejudiced views are not displaying psychopathological conflicts and weaknesses, but are merely living the ways of life they have learned in their society – which includes the family. The minimizing of social factors is dangerously likely to lead to a defeatist position, because although it is not yet within the power of the social sciences to undertake large-scale schemes of psychotherapy, we *can* tentatively suggest means of minimizing inter- (or intra-) group conflicts.

IV. REACTIONS TO MINORITY STATUS: IS THERE A MARK OF OPPRESSION?

It has been suggested here that there is a relationship between patterns of upbringing and personality, and that we might, therefore, observe that members of minority groups behave somewhat differently from majority group members. Further, the upbringing of prejudiced and non-prejudiced people differs in some important respects.

It is sometimes plausibly argued that an *inevitable* consequence of belonging to a minority group is that the individual develops psychopathological traits characteristic of that group. Elkins (1963) actually goes to the extent of tracing an analogy between the experiences of detainees in German concentration camps and those of Negro slaves, though he admits that such an analogy is a 'risky business'.

The dangers of arguing too strongly that minority status influences personality directly and in the direction of distorting personality from 'normality' are:

1. There is a danger of describing partial and biased stereotypes. *The* Negro is as useless a concept as *the* white. *The* Jew is as much a fiction as *the* anti-Semite.

2. Further, some characteristics of minority-group membership are not directly due to that status but to other factors, for instance, to membership of a lower class, or to domicile in a poor neighbourhood. Rosen (1959) has demonstrated that lower-class Negroes are poorly motivated for education and have a high proportion of drop-outs, truancy, etc. But this pattern is found equally among non-Negro lower-class young people and children.

3. 'What value stands are stated or implied in the study of personality?' (Simpson and Yinger, 1965). Usually the values chosen or implied are those of the majority group, and there is an implicit assumption of the inferiority of minority-group members.

Biesheuvel (1959), for example, commits this error in his lecture on 'Race, culture and personality', in the context of South Africa. He claimed to be making 'a contribution to the psychology of African personality', and having begun by asserting his belief in the 'undeniable, overt, and unalterable fact of biological difference', he proceeded to draw a fantastic, value-loaded picture of urban African communities and their inhabitants. He said that

'although these location dwellers are not entirely devoid of culture, they come near to being so, and the evidence in support of the view that instinctive urges dominated their behaviour is to be found in the lawlessness and violence. . . .

'In many ways, it is reminiscent of the early Renaissance . . . like the Elizabethan, the African looks out on a mysterious world, but that, unlike the former, he is unable to act out his inner turmoil by means of war, discovery and adventure. . . .'

Biesheuvel's evidence is a spicy scrap of journalism, impressionistic and second-hand. But even were the observations accurate and reliable, Biesheuvel appears to assume that *the* standard of culture is that of non-African urban societies in Africa. The asserted deviation from this standard is stigmatized by instinctive urges and filled with turmoil.

4. The *causes* of observed or reported differences are rarely adequately analysed. And most rare is the attempt to trace a connection between changes in personality characteristics and changes in the experiences of the group.

'Slowly, imperceptibly, the frame of reference for many Negro Americans has shifted during the past few decades . . . the rising expectations of the present are increasingly framed in terms of the wider society.' (Pettigrew, 1964.) Although the basic position of inferior status of the Negro has not radically changed, the psychological consequences of the changes in his status – particularly in education, urbanization and occupation – are attracting too little attention from psychologists.[1]

One of the most persuasive (if most impressionistic) analyses of the consequences of minority-group status is Mannoni's study of the psychology of colonization: *Prospero and Caliban.* This book has as its basic object the analysis of

'the meeting of two entirely different types of personality and their reactions to each other, in consequence of which the native becomes "colonised" and the European becomes a colonial.'

He argues that the assimilation of 'European' culture by 'native' culture (1) can succeed only if the 'personality' of the native is first destroyed through uprooting, enslavement and the collapse of the social structure; (2) causes 'the celebrated inferiority complex of the coloured peoples', which is 'the key

[1] Compare Davis, A., and Dollard, J., *Children of Bondage* (Harper Torchbooks, 1964, originally published in 1940), with the follow-up: Rohrer, J. H., and Edmondson, M. S., *The Eighth Generation Grows Up* (Harper Torchbooks, 1964, originally published in 1960).

to the psychology of backward peoples, and their relationship of dependence upon the "European" '; (3) is hampered by the difficulty that 'it is not yet clear how a personality originally constructed on the "non-civilized" model can later produce a second, "civilized" personality' (Mannoni, 1964).

Mannoni's materials are drawn from Madagascar during and immediately after the revolt of 1947 in which 80,000 Malagasy were killed, and as a result of which unexpected upheaval the French had to reconquer the island. But his analytic approach appears to be based upon a curious, eclectic *mélange* of Jungian, Kleinian and Adlerian ideas.

Mannoni distinguishes the 'native' and the 'civilized' personality, and with the aid of florid quotations and a strained interpretation of a speech by Caliban, suggests that the colonized peoples have *no* personality at all.

> 'Ariel, Friday, Caliban, the cannibals. . . . Nothing outside themselves affects them. After all, what sorts of personalities have Miranda, Ariel or Friday? None at all, so long as they remain submissive. Caliban, it is true, asserts himself by opposing, but he is mere bestiality.'

The 'inferiority complex' of colonized peoples springs, according to Mannoni, from differences in skin colour that the coloured person perceives as disadvantageous: associated with white are power, privilege and status. But this 'inferiority complex' operates only where another complex, 'the dependence complex', fails to operate, i.e. when the 'bonds of dependence [of the colonized people upon the colonizers] are in some way threatened'. This dependence is 'the key to the psychology of backward peoples', and accounts for their belief in magic and elucidates what seems to whites at first sight incomprehensible in the psychological reactions of the colonized. Mannoni illustrates this by considering the giving of gifts or services by a 'European' to a 'native'. A relationship develops in which the colonized individual 'appears to feel that he has some sort of claim upon the European who did him a kindness', and he returns to make further demands as an 'outward and visible sign of this reassuring relationship of dependence'. If this view be correct, it follows that the colonized people suffer greatly and are in danger of personality disintegration if they are threatened with abandonment by the colonizers – just as a child who is over-dependent upon his parents suffers if the family breaks and he is abandoned.

In one of the very few cross-cultural applications of his argument, Mannoni refers to observations on Africans of Westermann who claimed that no African suffers from an inferiority complex because

> 'within his own circle he is never in a position where he does not know how to behave or what to do. . . . This consciousness that one is surrounded by friends and can always rely upon their support helps to give everyone both in his attitude to life and in his manner that self-reliant assurance which strikes everyone as so pleasing in the "uncivilized" African.' (Westermann, 1949.)

A view which returns to the sentimental oversimplifications of eighteenth-century portrayals of the 'noble savage'.

Finally, Mannoni asserts that the dead and the ancestors occupy a considerable place in the formation of 'primitive' personality, and that this place comes to be occupied by the colonizer – whether or not he appreciates that this reinforces the dependence of the colonized people upon him.

The most fundamental defect of Mannoni's plausible argument is its precarious connection with observable data. Nowhere in *Prospero and Caliban* does Mannoni attempt a systematic survey of personalities of colonized and colonizers with particular reference to dependence-independence. Mannoni might have written his study equally well without having lived nearer to Madagascar than Gare St Lazare. Ignoring the need for methodical surveys of the behaviour of colonized and colonizers, he blinds himself to the very wide differences in social structure and social relationships in different colonies both within and between colonizers and colonized. A theory that attempts to draw, say, both pre-1948 India and pre-1964 Zambia – or 1968 South Africa – into one schema is so over-simplified as to explain little or nothing.

Mannoni's argument, however eloquent, is dubious:

1. He starkly opposes two antithetical groups: 'the native' and 'the European'. No reputable psychologist would accept Mannoni's assumption that there is a valid psychology of

peoples by which it is possible to compare 'the native' and 'the European' mind. No study exists that can confidently be taken to describe the characteristics of any large group of people – there is much individual variation within so small a group as a family, let alone a social class or a nation or a race. It is only possible to make global comparisons between groups, if these are made in sweeping terms and about comparatively trivial matters, but the more detailed the studies of a group, the more individual differences appear, and the more easy it is to find some similar individuals in another group. Put curtly: many natives have European minds, and some Europeans will have native minds – if by this is implied insight into, and sympathy and identification with, members of the other group.

2. Mannoni ignores the determination with which the colonizer has striven to create and to maintain a relationship of dependence upon him, and the reluctance of many colonized peoples to accept this relationship. The colonizer wants to be the one adult in a world of children: there is little evidence that the colonized also want this world. The colonizer easily deceives himself that this dependency relationship is a major characteristic of the colonial situation, particularly where this fits into the economic and political needs of colonialism.

3. Mannoni's central argument is that the need to be dominated and the accompanying feelings of inferiority inescapably develop when the sense of dependence is threatened. But the analogy upon which this argument is based is grotesquely oversimplified. The child's role within the family and the role of the colonized adult within a colonial situation are only superficially alike. Mannoni ignores the major difference that the family is the only world of the child, whereas the colonized peoples had a history and may still have the vestiges (or possibly much) of their pre-colonial social system, values, religion and myth. Colonized people are often forced to relinquish their past, and even where this force appears to succeed, some elements of the past influence the present. There seems to be little means short of the physical destruction of a people to destroy their culture. For example, the Jews have retained a remarkable cultural identity and psychological independence, despite their decimation in recent times, and even the uprooted West Africans who formed the majority of slaves in the West Indies and North

America are now believed to be less de-cultured than was once held.

Unlike many children, therefore, many colonized peoples have had something to fight for – their culture, wealth and lands, and their people. But were Mannoni to be correct, there would be little reason why the cosy dependence of colonization should ever be rejected, or why colonization has been so long resisted in Asia, and Africa. It could moreover be argued with equal cogency that the disappointment of the sense of dependence need not result in feelings of inferiority. A sudden and traumatic breach of the bonds of dependence can – and sometimes does – act as a catalyst stirring the individual to a maturer vigour, that seemed before no part of his personality.

If it is a psychological truism that 'a strongly developed ego gives a sense of personal control and personal responsibility for important events in one's life' (Havighurst, 1970), then one would expect that if circumstances permit or encourage control and responsibility the ego would develop more healthily. The recent political activity of American blacks has, therefore, favourable psychological implications – as well as some less favourable. Coles (1968, 1968a) in his psychiatric studies of the effects of school desegregation has reported how both white and black adolescents and younger children significantly change their attitudes towards each other in desegregated schools. In particular, most of the black children experienced no psychiatric harm and managed with reasonable success their new educational and social problems.

The few studies of personality formation in colonial or formerly colonial peoples show a picture that is far more complex than that drawn by Mannoni. In Africa, Albino and Thompson (1956) for example, meticulously traced the effects upon Zulu babies of sudden weaning, and found that, far from the babies clinging supinely to their mothers, the traumatic weaning often accelerated emotional maturity and independence. A major factor involved would seem to be interest shown by even distant members of the family in the child's efforts to act in a more grown-up fashion. In a study recently made by the writer in Zambia[1] a large sample of young adults

[1] Study unpublished at time of writing.

and adolescents overwhelmingly agreed that their future depended upon themselves, and not upon external circumstances, and in assessing the relevant external circumstances showed as much wisdom and realism as European students. Less than half specified their marriage partner or their friends. About the same proportion said that their future would be determined by their education, career or ambition. A quarter (not unreasonably) mentioned the policies of government, political stability (particularly the situation in Rhodesia and South Africa), and an insignificant number believed that events in the Bible would determine the future.

What of their general feelings about the future? A bare 10% felt indifferent or resentful and, of these, most mentioned the war in Nigeria and the situation in Rhodesia and South Africa. The majority of the remainder felt either hopeful or enthusiastic, and a few felt both.

Mannoni's analysis depends heavily upon the supposition of dependence-relationship of colonized peoples towards whites, but the writer found that spontaneous autobiographies supplemented by detailed questionnaires failed to reveal these dependence-needs among his Zambian informants. Although all but a tiny number were aware early that they were Africans and not white (mostly at six years or earlier), and though all were aware of the disadvantages of not being white, there was no indication of morbid self-pity or dependence or unreal reluctance to face the consequences of being African. The reported distinctions between Africans and whites (in descending order of frequency) were segregation; difference in social and economic life; physical appearance (far behind); language; and fear, envy or a harsh incident. One young woman became aware at eight that she was not the same as white children, and reported being made aware 'when my European friend was not allowed to have food at our home ... when she was not allowed to go swimming with us African girls ... when my friend's mother *in my presence* scolded her and told her never to bring African friends home because they are dirty and have no manners'.

These young men and women showed few or no signs of the passivity and sense of inferiority that the history of their nation should (according to Mannoni's analysis) have encouraged.

Like the Malagasy, they had lived during most of their lives in an authoritarian white-dominated society which daily demonstrated their economic, technological and social inferiority. They were all but a tiny handful educated in authoritarian white-dominated mission-schools, and were living in a highly insulated university that perpetuated the appearance (and a considerable part of the substance) of white (now called 'ex-patriate') domination. They had often heard from their elders accounts of the slave-trading times, the wars against colonizing invaders and of the defeat of African societies by the technically more sophisticated whites. It is the writer's impression of Africans (particularly in and from Southern Africa) that they show little morbid passivity. Indeed, neither Mannoni nor any other psychologist has attempted to analyse the precise combination of readiness to dominate and propensity to subordination which would bring about the situation that Mannoni regards as universal. Neither is there much information and analysis of the contrary situation, a colonized people spiritually resisting even when the objective odds against their beating the colonizers are very high.

But even were Mannoni's descriptions accurate, an alternative analysis is possible – and more plausible. Mannoni fails to probe for the motivations behind social behaviour. It is likely that much of the conformity of the colonized person, and his acceptance of the situation of colonialism are simple, superficial defences masking an inner seething hostility. Certainly the resistance to slavery and colonial domination has been no support of Mannoni's view. Mannoni asserts that it is difficult to understand how 'a personality originally constructed on the "non-civilized" model can later produce a second "civilized" personality'. The conflict supposed by Mannoni will vanish when the society itself is integrated. Any man who lives in a changing culture may have conflicts and loyalties tugging him in different directions; but most men and women are adaptable and stable enough to meet the challenge of their times without disintegration. The social psychological problem is less that of changing individual men and women, than of adapting social institutions to satisfy individual needs.

Gustav Jahoda (1962) criticizes Mannoni in an empirical study of the attitudes of Africans in Ghana towards Europeans

75

before and after independence. He makes two main criticisms: (1) Mannoni probably over-estimates the place the colonizer occupies in the minds of the colonized people; and (2) he exaggerates the emotional contrast between the dependent Malagasy and the 'free and independent' adult European.

Jahoda's own researches show clearly that the attitudes of the Africans towards Europeans are as mixed as the attitudes of any groups towards another with which it had been in long contact. Among secondary schoolboys, for example, Jahoda found evidence of

'two diametrically opposite pulls: on the one hand the influence of Western norms and values, usually inextricably confounded with the achievements and norms of the whites in which they were taken as being embodied; on the other hand, some antagonism to whites arising from the former colonial situation, and linked with this an assertion of the worth of African personality and culture engendered by the rising tide of nationalist feeling.'

Another very different view from that of Mannoni is that of the Algerian psychiatrist Fanon. He too argues that the colonizer and the colonized are two types of men, and that 'the colonial world is a world cut in two'. 'Decolonization is quite simply the replacing of a certain "species" of men by another "species" of men . . . there is a total, complete and absolute substitution.' (Fanon, 1965).

But Fanon takes the view that the colonized peoples, far from passively absorbing the values of the colonizer and assessing his conduct in the terms of the dominant group, rebel overtly or covertly.

'This is why the dreams of the native are . . . of action and of aggression. . . . I dream that I am jumping, swimming . . . that I span a river in one stride, or that I am followed by a flood of motor-cars which never catch up with me. During the period of colonization, the native never stops achieving his freedom from nine in the evening until six in the morning.'

When the colonial regime is coming to an end Fanon argues that 'violence is a cleansing force. It frees the native from his inferiority complex and from his despair and inaction; it makes him fearless and restores his self-respect.'

The Negro rioting in the USA is, from this point of view, both a political protest *and* a catharsis.

This suggests the questions: '*Is* there a mark of oppression?' 'Is a belief in racialism necessarily psychopathological?'

Kardiner and Ovesey (1962) published in 1951 'A psychological study of the American Negro', which reports their investigations of the former question. The authors made an intensive psychoanalytical study of twenty-five Negroes, drawn from various ages, social-economic classes and from both sexes. They frankly admit that their study was a pilot project and that it does not tell 'what comprises the personal adaptation of the successful Negro business man, the successful actress, the successful baseball player, the successful racketeer, and the like'. It is an attempt to draw a composite picture of Negro maladaptation to a caste situation.

In their case histories the authors found various syndromes, mostly elaborations of the attempt to reduce the tensions of low self-esteem. One pattern was the following projection: low self-esteem led to self-contempt, and this in turn to an idealization of whites. But the individual could not *be* white, although he might make "frantic efforts" to act as though he were. His efforts to be white being unattainable, and therefore disappointed, he comes to hate whites for having rejected him. But he still, unconsciously, identifies with the whites – his ideal reference group – and his hatred of whites becomes deflected against himself and against other Negroes. He hates himself for being black; he hates his fellow-Negroes because they are the evidence before him at every moment that he is black. Other forms of compensation were: apathy and a low level of aspiration and self-confidence; a shallow and (often frenzied) hedonism; "living for the moment"; and criminality.[1]

---

[1] Grier and Cobbs (1968), who are both black and psychiatrists also find that in their psychiatric practice a significant proportion of their black patients experience extreme frustration that may take the form of self-destructive anger and hate. One had a double hatred: of the society that forces blackness to be equated with inferiority, and one hates oneself, one's parents, one's race, for making one black and therefore vulnerable.

One of their interviewees, an ex-convict and drug-addict of considerable intelligence, was interviewed a month after his release from jail. He expresses well the complex of social and psychological tensions that combine to defeat many Negroes:

> 'A young kid growing up in Harlem, the only people he sees who have money are the pimps, the prostitutes, the people in the sporting world. So then maybe he go home and maybe his mother ain't working and he asks her for money and she ain't got none and maybe sometimes there ain't even no food. . . . A man got to be pretty strong to resist that temptation. . . . I just feel beat, that's all.'

It is significant that he refers to the mother as the earning parent and, therefore, the source for money and food. It is well-documented that the Negro working-class family is more frequently fatherless than other families in a similar socio-economic class.

Less impressionistic than Mannoni, Kardiner and Ovesey's study is a pioneering systematic attempt to apply the rational techniques of psychoanalysis to the investigation of social-

---

The recent emergence of the Black Panther (and other) movements concerned with the question 'Who are we, *really*?' may ultimately help restore to blacks some sense of satisfying identity, but there must inevitably be first a considerable explosion of rage against those who are perceived (albeit unconsciously) as the destroyers of one's identity and selfhood.

Another black psychotherapist, Calnek (1970), has carefully analysed the self-determination of black patients in therapy, and observes that many therapists and their patients try to avoid acknowledging that they are black, and that the patients' problems may be derived (in part or wholly) from his being black. Neither therapist nor patient can bear to face the fact of his blackness. Neither dare risk arousing his anger and self-hatred about his blackness.

Even research may be affected by this uncertainty of identity. Comer (1970) has discussed 'Research and the Black Backlash', and criticizes social scientists for ignoring that 'blacks were forced to make adaptive and defensive adjustments different from those of whites', and for interpreting behaviour as pathological, when it was 'normal' in the circumstances. Not surprisingly, Comer reports that many blacks are now refusing to be researched upon – they refuse to accept the implicit assumption of some social science research that there is something curious or pathological about being black, though there is, of course, a specific problem of adjustment to a hostile society if you are black.

psychological behaviour. But, despite its authors' good intentions, it is vulnerable to criticism: (1) How far does the tiny sample of patients reasonably represent the 11 million Negroes in the USA? The variety of social conditions in which Negroes live is barely suggested by the sample, and it is irrelevant to point out that all Negroes are Negroes first and members of this or that social or economic or cultural group secondly. The responses to these many and sometimes conflicting conditions are themselves the most important (and still largely unexplored) phenomena. (2) Kardiner and Ovesey's case-histories show so wide a range of personality responses (both normal and abnormal) that the reader is left with the unresolved question to tantalize him: precisely what combination of inner weaknesses and strengths, and external, social, pressures make one Negro marked by oppression and another steeled and toughened?

Indeed, Kardiner and Oversey ought to tell the reader why the Negroes can include as manifold a collection of human beings as, say, Kenneth B. Clark, the late Malcolm X, James Baldwin, Muhammad Ali and the brave woman who unwittingly began the Montgomery bus boycott, and many unknown men, women and children who suffer the indignities of being black in a discriminatory society but yet appear to cope in their everyday lives.

The questions therefore still have to be asked: How many Negroes *are* defeated? How does the proportion compare with that of other groups? Pettigrew (1964) summarizes and discusses the evidence: 'Negro incidence rates for psychosis [are] about twice as large as white rates. Particular psychoses contribute disproportionately . . . schizophrenia . . . paresis and alchoholic psychosis.' He found the group data on neurosis 'somewhat contradictory', but found that tentatively 'the ratio of Negro to white neuroticism is not as great as for the psychoses, and for certain other conditions, like character disorders, the Negro rate may actually be less than the white'. The findings on suicide are less equivocal. Negroes commit suicide 'far less frequently than whites . . . 1949 through 1951, [the Negro suicide rate] was only 42% of the white rate.'

A comparison with the data from South Africa suggests that the picture is highly complicated by sociological features of the situation of minority groups:

'At the end of 1962 there were 9,469 white and 15,076 non-white mentally disordered and defective persons under statutory care. . . . So far as non-whites were concerned, there was an excess of patients over beds of an average of 5,472. . . .

'The Commissioner [of Mental Hygiene] stated that the percentage of long-stay cases was higher for non-whites than for whites. The discharge rates, respectively, were 87% and 72%.' (Horrell, 1965.)

The South African Council for Mental Health reported in 1962 that there were between 500 and 600 non-white mental patients each month held in police cells awaiting medical treatment (*Race Relations News*, November 1962).

In South Africa there are approximately four non-whites to every one white; if therefore figures for mental patients were in the same proportion, there would be nearly 38,000 non-white mental patients, i.e. more than twice the 1962 figure.

What are some of the causes of these differences? No authority would take the view that they are 'racial'. Genetic, constitutional factors possibly create a sensitivity to severe schizophrenic disorders, but most authorities agree that among all races there is roughly the same potential for mental illness. It is to the social situations that one must look. In the USA and in South Africa, the social differences between the upper and lower classes are marked: poorer education, more ill-health, overcrowding, more unemployment and the resultant insecurity in homes broken by migration in search of work, where the role of adult males is inferior. Further, Negroes in the USA and non-whites in South Africa are rarely able to afford hospitalization except in the gravest circumstances, and therefore will tend to swell the figures of the psychotic patients. Social class is then a part of the explanation, and Pettigrew draws an interesting parallel between the cases of the American Negro, the Peruvian *mestizo* and the changing situation of Jewish Americans. The Peruvian *mestizo* scrapes a bare living in the slums on the edges of Lima, and among this group, alcoholism, family disorganization and mental illness are widespread. The Jewish American suffers from a different pattern of insecurity from the Negro, and suffers more often neurosis than psychosis. Pettigrew predicts that as the position of the Negro changes, 'the ambiguous, discrete rejection of the future may well lead to an increase of neuroticism among Negroes, as it has among Jews . . . psychosis rates will begin to recede as neurosis rates climb steadily.'

V. RACE AWARENESS AND ABNORMALITY

It should now be clear that the prejudiced or ethnocentric person is not necessarily suffering from a mental illness, nor need he even be regarded as a potential sufferer. He is often a normally well-adjusted person who accepts cultural norms of prejudices and ethnocentricism.

Nor should it be too lightly assumed that the 'mark of oppression' is a direct and inevitable consequence of minority group membership. Members of groups suffering from discrimination and prejudice often maintain a tough grasp on reality and do not show marked symptoms of mental abnormality.[1]

On the 'mark of oppression' it should be noted that although an oppressed group might fail to find status-satisfaction in certain areas of living, they might find psychologically adequate satisfactions in other areas, or even withdraw from the conflicts into beliefs in a millennial religion or political belief. The statistics of mental disturbance do not, in themselves, offer any indication of whether or not an oppressed group is more susceptible to neuroses or psychosis because of its minority position. The 'mark of oppression' is, possibly, a mark that is not peculiar to a racial group but to many 'underdogs', and is, therefore, a mark that rising status and lessening uncertainty will tend to erase.

Knupfer (1947) in her 'Portrait of the Underdog' shows how economic underprivilege leads to psychological uncertainty, the habit of submission, ignorance and a reluctance to participate in 'many phases of our predominantly middle-class culture'. In Africa, where Africans have suffered repression,

---

[1] For instance, the observations of a psychoanalyst imprisoned in a Nazi concentration camp: Bettelheim, B., 'Individual and mass behaviour in extreme situations', *J. Abn. Soc. Psychol.* 1943, **38,** 417–52. Also Lifton, R. J., *Thought Reform and the Psychology of Totalism:* a study of 'brain-washing' in China, 1961, New York, W. W. Norton.

violence and social disruption more severe than that which the American Negroes have suffered, there seems little evidence of unusually widespread or abnormally severe personality disorganization. Nor is the evidence of other minority groups in the USA unambiguous.

The 'mark of oppression' is often perilously close to an argument in biological racial terms. All minority groups are vulnerable. The combination of economic and social deprivation, the inability to create a viable (though minority) culture, the lack of political and ideological cohesion, the conflict between the desire for social acceptance and the rejection by the majority groups do, indeed, place great stress upon an individual. But many individuals do succeed in creating for themselves an alternative life that satisfies them adequately.[1]

An equally tangled issue is the relationship between mental health and prejudice. On the one hand Levison reports in *The Authoritarian Personality* that she found personality differences between highly prejudiced, unprejudiced and mildly prejudiced patients that were diagnostic of some major differences between the 'normal' and 'abnormal' personalities. But Marie Jahoda (1960) prefers the more moderate view that 'prejudice is related to the absence of positive mental health'. In other words, the prejudiced person suffers from diminished mental health, which is by no means the same as suffering from a mental disturbance. Some prejudiced persons *will* show a deep emotional need to be prejudiced; others will show little sign of mental conflict, anxiety and other criteria of mental illness.

Pettigrew has sought to estimate the relative importance of personality and social factors in attitude formation. Comparing the prejudice of white South Africans against Africans with anti-Negro prejudice in the Southern USA, he concludes that:

'In areas with historically imbedded traditions of racial intolerance, externalizing personality factors underlying prejudice remain important, but sociocultural factors are unusually crucial and account for the heightened racial hostility.' (Pettigrew, 1958.)

The South African sample consisted of one-third of the student body of the mainly English-speaking student body of

[1] See Roach and Gurrslin, 1967.

the University of Natal in Durban. These students showed evidence of considerable hostility towards Africans, and they mostly accepted the *apartheid* ideology. Yet, their responses to measurements of authoritarianism showed little difference from American student populations. Therefore, these South African students were sharply prejudiced yet they showed no marked personality factors to account for their extreme intolerance. The relevance of socio-cultural factors is emphasized by the data. For instance, the 560 students who were born in Africa were no more authoritarian than the other students, but they were significantly more intolerant. And the English-speaking students were less intolerant than the Afrikaans-speaking, but were not significantly less authoritarian. Pettigrew's comparative analysis of American whites supports this finding.[1]

VI. CONCLUSION

The essential problem of the social psychologist concerned with the development of personality and attitudes is the articulation of the social and the individual factors in development. What are the individual and social mechanisms by which men and women achieve a workable normality in circumstances that to an observer seem unpromising? Many – possibly the majority – answer the questions, 'Who am I?' and 'How do I fit into the world?' in a relatively satisfactory fashion.

There are contrasting dangers arising from assuming an exclusively sociological or psychological approach. Writers who over-emphasize social and cultural influences tend to exaggerate the psychological vulnerability of Negroes, colonized peoples and others of low status who live in a discriminatory and depriving society. The individual is readily assumed to be highly malleable and self-destructively sensitive to the stress and conflict of his sub-society. Moreover, it may be objected that there is much individuality in the perception of hostile, threatening or constricting environments, and individual styles are developed to meet threat and constriction.

[1] For accounts of student attitudes in South Africa, see Bloom, L., 'Self Concepts and Social Status in South Africa', *J. Soc. Psychol.*, 1961, **54,** 3–12; Danziger, K., 'Self-interpretations of Group Differences in Values (Natal, South Africa)', *J. Soc. Psychol.*, 1958, **47,** 317–25; Danziger, K., 'Validation of a Measure of Self-rationalisation', *J. Soc. Psychol.*, 1963, **59,** 17–28.

Even in such destructive situations as living in prison or con-centration camps, men and women succeed in creating a viable ego, and minimize instability or marked psychopathology.

On the other hand, to overemphasize the development of individual attitudes and to minimize the social influences ignores that many ethnocentric people are normally well adjusted to their societies. It obscures the apparent ease with which ethnocentric and tolerant attitudes can be learned with as little conflicts as are involved in learning a language or other socially defined skill.

Chapter 4

THE PROBLEM OF
RACE RELATIONS IN
GREAT BRITAIN

In 1634 the court painter, Van Dyck, portrayed Queen
Henrietta Maria and a 'blackamoor', the latter gorgeously
clothed and bejewelled in dramatic contrast to the chalky
beauty of the Queen. Henrietta Maria's 'blackamoor', though
a servant, was no menial. He had the charismatic attraction of
the unfamiliar, but he was neither a freak nor an exotic pet.
As early as the fourteenth century Chaucer had written about
Auffrike, and Eldred Jones (1965) has collected a strikingly
long list of 'plays, masks and pageants involving African
characters' from 1510. Shakespeare has many references to
Africa, and portrays several Moors, both 'tawny' and black,
and is from time to time idyllic about the recently opened
continent. Ancient Pistol, for example, was no sentimentalist,
and his sigh, 'I speak of Africa and golden joys' has been
echoed through the centuries by tough-minded fishers for
souls, land or profits, who came to exploit Africa and were
bewitched by its boisterous charms.

Othello, the magical Moor, was a man 'great of heart'
and in no way a caricature. Shakespeare, genius though he
was, could never have written the plea

'When you shall those unlucky deeds relate,
Speak of me as I am; nothing extenuate,
Nor set down aught in malice;'

unless he felt that the Elizabethan audience accepted Othello
as a fellow human being despite his darker skin and unusual
appearance.

Although 'coloured' people never vanished from literature

85

and art in the UK probably until about the early nineteenth century, they were too few to be widely feared, resented and resisted. Queen Elizabeth's edict for the transportation of Negroes out of England in 1601 seems to be based on fear of commercial rivalry rather than on modern racialism. And Foot (1965) in his study of *Immigration and Race in British Politics* opens his historical chapters in 1886, when members of both the Tory and the Liberal Parties were professing anxiety about the 'nihilists' and Jews from Eastern Europe who were moving westwards (mostly to the USA) to escape pogroms and persecution. The political and social repercussions of slavery, colonialism and imperialism from time to time aroused interest and concern, even throughout the eighteenth century, but it is doubtful if race relations and race attitudes played a major part in social and political life in England until the early nineteenth century. A series of slave revolts preceded the abolition of slavery in 1833, and the attitudes towards the Irish 'navigators' who dug the canals and built the railroads from the 1830s were crudely racialistic. Not until 1905 was an issue of race a major political event. In that year Balfour committed the political error of endorsing the importation of 'indentured' Chinese 'coolies' to work on the mines on the Reef, and the Liberal Party issued a highly effective leaflet accusing the government of encouraging 'Chinese slavery'. The recently formed Labour Representation Committee predicted dangers to organized labour if cheap, non-union workers were allowed, and the uproar was so loud that Ensor (1949) considered that this issue alone could have caused the defeat of the government.

By 1967 the 'colour problem' seemed to have become so intense that confrontations of immigrant organizations and the police (as representatives of the established law) were a matter for wide concern. In November 1967, for example, the third annual convention of CARD (Campaign Against Racial Discrimination) was held, and among the statements issued was one that regretted that

'one of the most disturbing features of our work is the extent to which we are inundated with complaints about the behaviour of the police. . . . The Home Secretary knows the extent of our concern at the deterioration in the relationship between the Coloured community and the police.' *Sunday Times*, 5 November 1967.)

During the same month this organization demonstrated in Islington (North London) and Moss Side (Manchester) against alleged brutality by local police, and called for a government enquiry into allegations of police misconduct and for the establishment of a review board independent of the police to hear complaints against them. Is there a parallel here with the accusations often made in the East End of London in the turbulent years before World War II, that local fascist toughs were favoured by the police, and protesting Jewish (and non-Jewish) residents were treated harshly and unfairly? Are the police reflecting a tendency for British political life to shift in the direction of racial prejudice?

Other indications of the tenseness in race relations are in the reports of Race Relations Boards, and in the charges brought against offenders contravening the Race Relations Act, 1965.

In Glasgow, for example, the Race Relations Board in its first eighteen months received some 600 complaints, of which most were about alleged discrimination in public houses. Only 176 of the complaints were within the scope of legislation, and the remainder concerned employment. The Board considered that the rate of complaints was growing. In the first thirteen months the Board received 327, but in the following five months almost another 300 (*The Times*, 10 August 1967).

The expression of racial hostility has at times exploded in group violence. The most notorious examples have been murderous riots shortly after World War I, in Cardiff and other ports with a large coloured population, anti-Jewish riots in the 1930s, and anti-coloured mobs in Notting Hill and the Midlands in the late 1950s. But individual expressions, apparently by pathologically disturbed men or women, are depressingly more frequently reported. In January 1968 an outbreak of violence against Jews and synagogues culminated in charges of conspiracy, and more recently charges have also been brought against coloured men and against Africans. One case involved men who in Hyde Park made speeches on behalf of the Universal Coloured People's Association, in which they said, 'The only way black people can emancipate themselves is to burn the white man's house', and members of the audience were advised to buy matches in order to burn them.

It is impossible to know if these (and other incidents) are symbolic of a major deterioration in race relations. We do not know, for example, if the complaints to Race Relations Boards indicate more than that people who formerly confined themselves to private grumbling and resentment, when provided with a forum for their complaints will convert them into litigation or quasi-litigation. On the other hand, the ethos of Britain does seem more permissive to the emergence of political parties such as the National Front of Andrew Fountaine, which openly advocates a British 'world system, based primarily on the white Commonwealth countries, plus South Africa', the repatriation of coloured immigrants, and 'unremitting support . . . to British and other European communities overseas in their maintenance of "civilization in lands threatened with a reversion to barbarism".' (*Sunday Times*, 25 February 1968.)

There is confusion among both the 'liberals' and the 'conservatives' in the field of race relations. The rubbish written in favour of a mythical race purity and the pleas to preserve the 'British way of life', are matched by the shrill exaggeration that

> 'the names of Sharpeville, Alabama, Mississippi, Notting Hill, Angola and the Congo have become symbols of the savagery of human passions.' (Hill, 1967.)

Nothing is gained by implying that the rioting in Notting Hill is comparable with the murders at Sharpeville; nor is the 'liberal' case strengthened by the gross assertion that the situation in the UK is so grave that 'nothing less than the future of Britain is at stake'.

II. FACTS AND FIGURES

Despite the concern with immigration, race relations (and related matters), the basic facts about the numbers of coloured, African, Indian and other 'non-white' peoples in the UK are difficult to discover, and often of doubtful reliability. This is partly because of the arbitrary vagueness of the terms 'coloured'

or non-white. In Britain it is puzzling to find that the word
'coloured' includes a spectrum ranging from Cypriots (occasionally) to the dark West Africans, by way of pale Ismailis,
and the inextricably mixed (in appearance) West Indians.
Many British citizens are 'coloured' in appearance but are in
every way culturally and socially as British as any European
immigrant whose forebears settled here generations ago. There
are in Cardiff, for example, many families whose origins are
now three dim generations ago in the West Indies or in West
Africa, and who are now entirely British in their culture and
allegiance.

In late 1966 a sample census of Great Britain found the
total population to be 52,303,720, of which only 6% had been
born elsewhere, i.e. slightly more than three millions. The census divided this immigrant population into three groups:
(1) those from other parts of the British Isles; (2) the Commonwealth; and (3) foreign, which includes Germany, Italy,
Poland, the USA, Russia, other parts of Europe, and 'other'.
By far the greater number of immigrants born elsewhere are
from Eire and Northern Ireland, who account for about one-
third. Of the rest about one-half come from the Commonwealth,
including an unexpectedly large number from Australia, New
Zealand and Canada, about 120,000, and about 100,000 from
the USA. The census estimated just over 300,000 Indians and
Pakistanis were born elsewhere, and about 270,000 West
Indians. By comparison, South Africa and Switzerland both
have about 12% of immigrants.

During the past ten years, the exaggerated concern with
migration has obscured the statistical picture, which does
not support arguments that Britain is in danger of flooding by
immigrants. In the years 1953–7 there was a net outflow from
Britain, and in the peak year for inflow (1961) the net inflow
was only 170,000, caused to a large extent by the rush of Commonwealth immigrants to enter before the controls of the 1962
Commonwealth Immigrants Act were enforced. In 1964 again
there was a net outflow, though only of 17,000, and laments
began about the 'brain drain' and the possibility of acute
labour shortages by 1970, when according to the National
Plan Great Britain might have a shortage of over 200,000
workers to fill.

The *total* of 'non-white' people in the UK has been estimated as just over 877,000 at the end of 1965, and their distribution by country of origin is:

British Caribbean	34%
India	30%
Pakistan	12%
Africa	8·5%
Cyprus	7%
Elsewhere	8·5%

The outstanding growth rate was 245% for Pakistanis between April 1961 and December 1965, but this was in raw figures only an increase of 32,000 to 110,553. The overall increases of 'non-white' people during this time was 73%, that is, from about 506,000 to 877,000.

Now, in the late 1960s, less than two out of every hundred residents of the UK are coloured, and barely six out of every hundred are from overseas. At the end of the century possibly four out of every hundred residents will be coloured, i.e. about 3 millions out of a total population of some 70 millions. But the population forecasts are notoriously unreliable. The immigrant birthrate is likely to fall as prosperity and education increases; the rate of net inflow will probably decline; the age structure of immigrants is unusual – a very high proportion of young people – and this peculiarity will correct itself, and there will be proportionately fewer women of child-bearing age among the coloured population. But above all, will these considerations matter by the end of the century?

'Fifty to seventy years ago, the immigration of Jews into this country was a burning issue, but how many Gentiles today – except for a minority – know or care how many Jews are living in England, or what their percentage is of the total indigenous population?' (Hooper, 1965.)

Not unreasonably, the immigrants tend to settle in large cities where there are jobs and social amenities, and where they will find other immigrants and possibly relatives. According to the census of 1961, Greater London has about 28 in every 100 of the coloured population, and far behind comes Birmingham with 7%. About 50% have settled in Britain's ten largest cities: London, Birmingham, Liverpool, Manchester, Leeds, Coventry, Sheffield, Nottingham and Bradford, and there are now nearly thirty towns or cities with a coloured population of an estimated 3,000 or more. The proportion of immigrants in neighbourhoods and cities varies widely, and panic on the right and protest on the left is easy to generate: fear of 'swamping' and fears of the creation of 'ghettoes'. In Wolverhampton, for example, of a total population of over 150,000, about 7,500 are West Indians, Indians and a few Pakistanis, and in 1965 Dr James Galloway, the MOH of Wolverhampton, reported that the town's coloured population was reproducing at a rate eight times as fast as that of other inhabitants. A similar report from Birmingham stated that the city had about 7,200 'non-white' citizens, that is, about 1 out of every 15, and that the immigrant birth-rate was 46 in every 1,000 births compared with the city average of 19·4.

None of the reports, however, mentions that these apparently alarming rates of increase amount to a very small number of babies added to the population every year.

In July 1969 the Institute of Race Relations published *Colour and Citizenship* (Rose, 1969), a massive report on race relations in the UK that draws together the evidence gathered during the Institute's five-year survey of the development and crystallization of patterns of race relations among the different communities, and in housing, education, employment and social life. At about the same time the Select Committee on Race Relations and Immigration published a four-volume report which, though entitled *The Problems of Coloured School-leavers*, in fact deals with broad problems of white and non-white immigrant youth and includes recommendations on education and employment.

Colour and Citizenship ends with some eighty pages of recommendations for future action, based upon the position that 'some form of additional official intervention is essential and that the policies so far undertaken have not proved adequate to the situation'. The need for a sense of urgency is the *leitmotif* of both the Institute's report and that of the Select Committee, and both agree that the so-called problem of colour cannot be treated in isolation from the general problems of poverty and urban decay.

A great part of the recommendations of *Colour and Citizenship* is concerned with administrative and governmental reorganization in order the more effectively to introduce and implement policies that on both a local and a national level might have the effect of encouraging acceptance of different groups on a social and cultural level, and in diminishing definable discriminatory practice. But one particular issue underlies all others: that of *dispersal*. Should it be policy to discourage the concentration of coloured people into quasi-ghetto areas? There is danger in too readily assuming that in the UK ghettoes have developed that bear comparison with those of the USA or South Africa; but there are tendencies for coloured people to become segregated in (often quite small) pockets in the poorer so-called 'twilight' areas of older industrial cities, where the disadvantages of low status, less adequate community facilities and social estrangement from the majority community are likely to be exacerbated. The survey warns of the danger that disadvantages can too easily be perpetuated and communities demoralized if geographical isolation leads to social and psychological insulation. If people, however, live close together to maintain their cultural or religious customs, but nevertheless are not afraid to move in the wider community, this is psychologically quite a different situation from where people are afraid to move within the city into what they fear – rightly or wrongly – to be a rejecting world. Bridges must be built between communities; the freedom of choice to move must be created and demonstrated.

The other major issues, education and employment, which fit into the broader framework of housing and urban development, are dealt with by the Select Committee, who pay much attention to the need for educational organizations from schools to teachers' training colleges to prepare children and young people to live in a multi-racial society, and make suggestions for the improvement of the youth services and youth employment offices. The Report also collated some suggestions for future research, mostly on aspects of the effects of educational arrangements on school performance, and including a plea for evaluation of methods of teaching race relations in schools in teachers' training colleges. 'Ignorance', concludes the Report, 'is our greatest enemy.' But the Report also implies that ignorance is created and encouraged in situations in which equality of status and of treatment are not afforded as of right.

III. THE EFFECTS OF IMMIGRATION: AREA STUDIES

Community studies of the impact of immigrants and hosts upon each other are beginning to become familiar, but surprisingly, the first large-scale study in Britain was not published until 1947, when Kenneth Little's anthropological account of the coloured community of Tiger Bay in Cardiff initiated a variety of studies of very varying quality. Even in 1967 a Register of Research on Commonwealth Immigrants (Sivanandan and Scruton, 1967), including both work in progress and unpublished theses, only reached 150 items by including some topics more relevant to medicine and education than to the broader field of race relations. It was not until 1958 that the Institute of Race Relations became an independent body – the first major attempt to coordinate the investigation of race relations in Britain. In 1963 the Survey of Race Relations in Britain was launched, initially as a counterpart of Gunnar Myrdal's massive *An American Dilemma*; but it developed into a loosely interrelated number of studies of housing, education, employment, health, public order, prejudice and discrimination, some based upon an intensive study of an area (e.g. Rex and Moore's study of Sparkbrook (Birmingham) and the writer's study of Cardiff), general accounts of a topic (e.g. Hepple's study of *Race, Jobs and the Law in Britain*, and Burney's researches into housing policies).

In this section three studies of areas will be outlined and discussed: Sparkbrook, Slough and Cardiff. Each is an independent investigation, focused about a particular set of problems. Sparkbrook is concerned with housing, Slough with the social dynamics of settling-in, and Cardiff with the attitudes towards the host population of white and non-white immigrants.

1. *Sparkbrook, Birmingham*

One of the most disturbing recent studies was of Sparkbrook—a multi-racial community in a 'twilight zone' of a large industrial city. The population is highly mixed: immigrants from Ireland, the West Indies and Pakistan live near by the original

English community, and are mingled with a notable number of English deviants of various kinds. Sparkbrook was found to have five types of housing, forming more or less distinguishable areas that ranged from old terraced working-class houses, often ready to be demolished, to commuter villages in rural or semi-rural surroundings. Intermediate zones are in stages of dilapidation and development. The most desired areas are those on the outskirts of the city, and the least desired are those areas in the centre from which the older-settled working classes are steadily moving away as their income and their status rises. Into these central areas coloured and Irish immigrants have tended to settle, forming a community of 'socially-disadvantaged' people living in poor and often overpriced housing, consisting largely of late Victorian middle-class houses converted into lodging-houses, crowded and depressing. The immigrants are therefore living mostly in areas of rapid decline, with bad quality housing, poor social amenities and great difficulties in improving their conditions.

Rex and Moore (1966) produce evidence that the creation of a quasi-ghetto is partially the responsibility of the housing policy of Birmingham City Council, who decided in 1968 that the city would neither revise its allocation scheme for housing nor redevelop the district. This decision was surprising for, as *The Times* observed: 'Birmingham was approaching a situation in which large areas of decaying property near the city centre would be inhabited by coloured immigrants while newer housing would be solidly white.'

To some extent this migration outwards from the city centre is a common feature of urban development and is found in many – if not all – cities, and the situation in Birmingham, though distressing, is not unique. However, Rex and Moore offer evidence that the formation of socially discrete areas is unwittingly in part caused by the city's housing policy. The authors estimated that by 1971 the housing shortage would be over 43,000 and even by 1980 it would still exceed 30,000. Allocating municipal housing must therefore be administered according to some principles, and the municipality must employ principles to govern their purchase and building of houses. A 'points' system was therefore devised which, while without any reference to skin colour, effectively excluded most immigrant families from the better class of housing provided or maintained by the city. The authors found no West Indians during their research who had been offered a council-built house, and there were very few coloured tenants in council housing estates. Both Irish and coloured immigrants were strongly convinced that even when they were qualified to have council housing they were offered inferior, patched-up older houses. The authors offer evidence that the city is unwilling to build in areas that have a high proportion of immigrants, and a scheme for Sparkbrook in July 1965 that would have rehoused 600 immigrant families was abandoned on the grounds that the Council was anxious to avoid creating a 'ghetto'.

But a ghetto exists, and the present policy seems destined – if not designed – to maintain it. Rex and Moore predict that near-slum and completely slum 'twilight zones' will spread, 'multi-occupation' and grossly overcrowded houses will increase in number, and the integration of immigrants into the wider community will continue slowly, haltingly and with needless (because avoidable)friction. Perhaps most disquieting is the observation that the immigrant is so low down in the local political power hierarchy, that he is almost totally excluded from influencing local politics. He pays his rates but he is powerless to choose policies that will help him. One West Indian JP is inadequate to ensure effective democratic participation by non-white rate-payers.

2. *Slough*

The major questions in this study were (a) the reasons why immigrants came to Slough: (b) their general reactions after they had settled there; and (c) the reactions to them of the host population.

The city of Slough, twenty miles from London, had in 1965 an estimated 7,000 coloured immigrants, i.e. 8% of the city's total population, most of whom came from the West Indies, India and Pakistan. A vigorous industrial city with an unusually alert and enlightened Council of Social Service, Slough seems to have less 'racialism' than many other cities with a similar proportion of non-white immigrants, and the host population seem to have been more welcoming and less hostile than other areas. The author (Israel, 1966) concluded that the high quality of local leadership and the prosperity of the area may be responsible for this comparatively satisfactory situation, and also commends the local press for their sober and unsensational reporting of news and comment about race problems. The police too seem to have taken pains to obtain the trust and respect of the immigrant groups.

The main attraction for immigrants was the fair opportunities for employment in a very wide range of jobs and skills. Many of the immigrants had friends and relatives already living in Slough, and the reassurance that there is a friend or relative who has already braved the unknown and who can point out the dangers to be avoided and the advantages to be sought, is probably as powerful an attraction as the often idealized and exaggerated economic prospects. The informal contacts between the immigrants and the host communities were reported as 'rather encouraging for prospects of social assimilation', but significantly, immigrants were more persistent than might be expected in pursuing these informal contacts. Neighbourhood contacts were 'slightly higher' than the investigator expected. Among all groups there was reported a slight increase in the intention to settle as the immigrant settled, and that except for a tiny sample of Pakistanis, there was a slight decrease in the decision not to settle. Few thought that their decision to come to the UK had been unwise or a mistake, and they comprised those who had had such difficulties as being unable to find accommodation or a job, or those who found the UK unhealthy. But few found that life in the UK was more enjoyable than life in the country they came from, for almost two-thirds of those interviewed thought that the British were prejudiced against non-white people, though barely 10% had actually suffered discrimination in Slough. Even in the field of employment 'the overall variety of job types seemed to compare favourably with the range of work done by the host community labour force', but very few immigrants thought that their opportunities for promotion and advancement equalled those of 'British' workers. A surprising two-thirds claimed to get along with their 'British' fellow-workers amicably, and many had very warm relationships.

The author of the Report encouragingly – and one hopes not too naïvely – was left with 'rather more cause for hope than despair': even so sensitive a social problem as housing failed to reveal wide prejudice in the sample interviewed.

A factor that Israel does not mention is the newness of Slough as an industrial city. This is not a city in transition. It has none of Birmingham's acute housing problems. It has been spared tendentious politicizing of the immigrant problem. Its local leadership has been sober, practical and firm.

3. Cardiff: 'Tiger Bay' and Bute Town[1]

This study was concerned with the psychological consequences of belonging to a minority group, mainly in and around Tiger Bay or Bute Town, the formerly flourishing dock area of Cardiff. It explores the styles of social and individual adjustment that have been formed in response to the condition (social and political) of white and non-white immigrants, and is particularly focused about the differences that exist between the third generation immigrants and more recent settlers. The findings are based upon an analysis of data obtained from some 330 interviews and two years of participant observation.

Cardiff provides an almost unique microcosm of the history of overseas settlement in Great Britain, both for the length of settlement and for the encapsulation of the majority of its immigrant population, which for more than three-quarters of a century has been isolated from the rest of the city, psychologically, socially and geographically.

The sample census of 1966 gave Cardiff a total population of about 254,000, of whom about 7,000 were of overseas origin. The non-white immigrant population is unknown, but has been estimated at about 3,300 – mainly West Indians but with some Pakistanis and Indians. But the figures are unreliable: an unknown number of citizens were born here and may be second or even third generation settlers; the total non-white population can only be guessed. Little (1947) estimated it was between 6,000 and 7,000, and possibly by 1967 it had increased to a

---

[1] Most of the material in this section is taken from my research in Cardiff, undertaken on behalf of the Institute of Race Relations' Survey of Race Relations in Britain, which was published in 1969. The bulk of the interviewing was most ably carried out by Mr D. J. Napal and Mrs B. Collins, without whose assistance – and encouragement – the project might not have been completed successfully.

G

maximum of about 8,000. The population is, therefore, unusually stable. Of a remarkable racial diversity, from light-skinned Muslim Arabs to very dark West Africans, the overwhelming majority of non-white people in Cardiff still cluster near to the moribund docks, and in the neighbouring Adamstown and Splott. But the white settlers are dispersed widely throughout Cardiff, and their distribution is not markedly different from that of other residents of a similar social-economic status.

Bute Town is not unfortunately a separate area for the purpose of the census, but is a major part of South Ward and the figures for South Ward can be confidently applied to the area without serious risk of distortion. Although the poverty of the inter-war years has vanished, the area is still a crowded, shabby and neglected-looking working-class neighbourhood, with a shortage of many facilities. In the 1961 census there was an average of 17·5 persons per acre, and 10·8% lived at more than 1·5 persons per room – which compared very unfavourably with the adjacent areas of Splott and Grangetown. In 1966, after the completion of a major part of the Council's rehousing programme, about 8% lived at more than 1·5 persons per room, but household amenities were still not adequate. There were still 30 households with no w.c., 620 with a shared outside w.c., over 1,000 with no fixed bath and nearly 1,000 with no hot-water taps. Less than one-half of the dwellings were owner-occupied, but the author found that only 23% of his non-white sample were owner-occupiers compared with nearly 69% of the whites, and of the non-white sample the proportion of those who owned their homes dropped sharply from 20% of the first generation to 11% of the second and to barely 8% of the third.

The insulated feeling of this peninsula is still noticeable. A Muslim informant who had lived in Cardiff for twenty-five years and could easily pass as white, commented to the author, 'Once you pass the lights in Bute Street and you're in white man's land'. The author found that a high proportion of the time of his non-white informants was spent within the area. There was less visiting outside the neighbourhood area than among the whites, and less frequent outings to the city for entertainments and recreation. In Bute Town there is little of the out-of-doors bustle and excitement often associated with

West Indian, Asian and African communities, such as one experiences along Kilburn High Road or 'down Portobello', but some of Cardiff's livelier clubs and night-life have taken over former commercial premises, with clients without any racial consciousness. A lingering handful of missions to seamen and the community and youth centres provide more conventional social and recreational facilities. The white settlers, mostly Italians and Greeks, are much more scattered, and have no area that they think of as their own. Except for attending their churches and such functions as weddings, they seem to have few regular meetings among their own communities.

The fundamental questions posed by the survey are centred about the identity of the immigrants: 'Who are we?' and the answers are to be found in the patterns of rejection and acceptance by the host community.

Some of the more general findings can be summarized:

Table One: Issues supported more by non-whites than whites

1. Coloured should try to preserve themselves as a race
2. Non-whites are more attractive than whites
3. Non-whites are superior to whites
4. Intermarriage is making the races closer together
5. Intermarriage would be good if only society would approve
6. Intermarriage is good if the partners choose it
7. Intermarriage is tough on the children because society disapproves
8. There is no such thing as a pure race – no racial differences really matter
9. If I were born white, I'd still be me – there'd be no difference.

The ambivalence of the non-whites was marked. They resisted any of the chauvinistic and paranoiac beliefs in race differences, and were acutely aware of the individual and social damage that crude racialism caused. Yet, they felt a pride in being coloured that was strongly tinged with regret that they were not, in the UK, free to feel both coloured *and* fully accepted as equal citizens to the English, who happened to have a different appearance (sometimes) and different [though not dissimilar) cultural background.

By comparison the white immigrants seemed to perceive themselves as different from both the host community and the coloured immigrants:

Table Two: Issues supported more by white than non-white

1. Whites and non-whites are separate races
2. White immigrants are a purer race than the 'local' whites
3. Whites are more attractive.
4. Differences exist between 'local' whites and immigrant whites in

    (a) Honesty   (d) Ways of life
    (b) Intelligence   (e) Opportunities
    (c) Education   (f) Physical appearance

More significant were the differences among the non-white immigrants from generation to generation:

Table Three

A: *Issues supported by more third-generation non-whites than generation one or two*

1. Intermarriage is making the races closer together
3. Neither whites nor non-whites are more attractive – it depends on the individual
3. Coloureds are superior to whites
4. Non-whites are purer in race than whites
5. I'd be better off if I were born white
6. Non-whites are more honest than whites

B: *Issues supported by more second-generation non-whites than generation one or three*

1. Intermarriage is good if the partners choose it
2. There are no differences between whites and non-whites
3. There is no such thing as a pure race – no racial differences really matter
4. I would be better off generally if I were white

C: *Issues supported by more first-generation non-whites than generation two or three*

1. Whites and non-whites are separate races
2. Coloured should try to preserve themselves as a race
3. Intermarriage is good if the partners choose it
4. Intermarriage is tough on the children because society disapproves
5. If I were born white, I'd still be me – there'd be no difference
6. Whites and non-whites are different: but one is superior in some and the other in other qualities
7. Whites are more attractive
(But paradoxically a few but not insignificant number held that:
8. Our own nation, e.g. Barbadians, are more attractive.)

Through the generations the ambivalence of the first generation is sharper, and more distressing to the individuals, than among the second or third. It is (in general) the first generation who have the most severe conflicts about who they are and what position they (and their children) can expect to occupy in the Britain which is to be their home. Tense, defensive, proud, yet with strong feelings that as coloured persons they are rejected and inferior, they have little reason to be confident that a stable quasi-ghetto like Cardiff's Bute Town is conducive to positive mental health and full social integration.

A *sense of self* only clearly emerged in Bute Town, and even where former residents, coloured and white, left to live in better quality areas, they often drifted back to visit friends and for an evening's entertainment. Only the small Pakistani group had both the spatial and social cohesiveness that seems necessary to give individuals a strong sentiment of belonging. The Italian's for example, dispersed throughout Cardiff have little to hold them together except language and religion, and are less a community than the Cypriots and Maltese in London. They feel themselves to be Italians, but want to be accepted by the host community. They gave the impression of achieving a notable degree of harmony between their Italianness and their Welshness. The Italians seemed integrated and rooted, speaking fluent English, playing a major part in the economic life of both Cardiff and South Wales, retaining as lively an interest in Italian food and culture as in such Cardiff interests as Rugby. Other white groups, the Greeks for example, seem less integrated. All missed the crowded intimacy, the gregariousness and the human and physical warmth of the Mediterranean, but few would wish to return.

A typical comment about living in Bute Town is similar to the stereotype often heard about 'working class' areas: a coloured woman now living in Ely (a pleasant working-class estate) missed Bute Town because

> 'It was so friendly. . . . They'd always offer you a cup of tea or something. . . . Nobody ever says you no. . . . We always kept our front doors open, but they're not used to that up here. First time I did it, they come and told me: "Your door's open". It wan't loneliness, but fear why they came and told me. . . .'

It was found that there was a tendency for Bute Town folk to settle into a ghetto-like existence. This was most marked among those who had lived a short while in Cardiff, but those who were born in Cardiff seemed to have both wide friendships and a strong sense of community.

Distance from the host population differed markedly between the different groups. Many non-white immigrants had idealistic valuations of the whites and were disappointed in their expectations. They had wanted to be friends, to be close, to be accepted, and were able to satisfy none of these longings.[1] The whites were 'disappointed guests' less frequently than non-white immigrants. Few expressed the bitterness of a young Nigerian who said:

'My coming here has made me realize certain misconceptions. The beliefs that we hold in our own country aren't valid. At home we feel the white man has all the attributes that are good, but now I find that some are worse than my own people – they are not as good as I imagined. . . . Whites cannot understand . . .'

He was shocked that the tribalism that his own people are struggling against was as violently and fruitlessly expressed by the British. No informant relished his insularity and distance from the host population. It was perceived as an unhappy and regrettable consequence of the insecurity of being non-white in a white city. Paradoxically, more of the whites interviewed would find it unpleasant to have intimate social contact with the host population than the non-whites. The West Indians were particularly sustained in a resolute indifference to 'colour' by moral, religious and political beliefs, and by a possibly idealized view of the racial mixing and harmony of the West Indies. Broadly, both for whites and coloured, there was a steadily decreasing social distance with the length of time lived in the UK. But few overt race prejudices were either stated or inferred. Linguistic and religious reasons were often given for reluctance to 'mix' socially, and a handful of Asians still felt themselves bound by caste.

The nature and quantity of contact between immigrants and hosts was remarkably varied between both groups and from

[1] It is not difficult to find confirmation of this. See, for examlpe, the autobiographical *Journey to an Illusion – The West Indian in Britain*, by Donald Hinds (Heinemann, 1966) and Henri Tajfel and John L. Dawson (editors), *Disappointed Guests* (Oxford, 1965).

individual to individual. But throughout the sample interviewed ran the theme – held naïvely or charitably – that understanding would increase only with social contact. A Mauritian man argued that

'Whites should go into the houses of coloured people and find out how we live. They ask us questions "Do you use knives and forks?" . . . If they looked further afield and discovered what a coloured person really is, *human* attitudes might change. . . .'

And the white immigrants agreed. A mildly pessimistic Italian woman said:

'There's good and bad in every country, but we are all so clannish. We cannot possibly understand how other people live. If we did we wouldn't be so bigoted. . . .'

But where does one make a first, informal contact? Large social gatherings are often embarrasing and discouraging, and contact at work does not necessarily encourage contact elsewhere. A Pakistani steel-worker observed that

'We all have some friend, but they have to be stubborn to be friends with us. . . . At work we drink tea, play cards and have a friendly punch-up. But in civilian clothes in the street, they pretend they don't know us. . . .'

Not surprisingly a minority of informants (31% of the non-whites and 45% of the whites), while approving in general terms of the benefits of contact, made reservations; and the more socially integrated community of Bute Town revealed fewer reservations.

Were *racial attitudes* realistic or resigned? It is difficult to distinguish. Without accepting as just or inevitable the discrimination and prejudice that they alleged, the informants nevertheless believed that one must make the best of this life and work to improve life for the next generation. The coloured informants were highly ambivalent about their colour. They expressed pride in being 'black' but felt acute dissatisfaction about what being black entails, and over 25% of those who had lived in the UK more than twenty years wished they had been born white.

And why not? 'You get a better deal in this world if you're white' – a pragmatic view that is irrefutable.

Few admitted that their experiences had made them anti-white or anti-British and bitter: only 4% of the non-whites and 1 per cent of the whites. But 7% of the non-whites felt 'disappointed' and about 10% had become warier and more cautious in their informal dealings with whites. Far fewer of the whites felt similarly. The non-whites were more hurt than angry, but the depth of feeling was as poignant as it was sincere. A man from St Kitts was pessimistic, as many non-whites and few whites were:

> '. . . I can't see this thing [racialism] finishing or dying out. When I settled here, I was surprised: I didn't expect it. . . . Now I've got to know that whatever happens there's still a little something in the white man against me. Even my friends: they'll go so far and no farther. . . . Something is held back. . . .'

In general the coloured informants tended more often than the whites to maintain that there were no differences between themselves and the 'host' population that changing circumstances could not alter, and it became clear early during the investigation that this was an aspect of the strong antipathy to any suggestion that racial differences existed. The non-white informants agreed that some differences resulted from different ways of life and from discrimination against immigrants. Opportunity and education were stressed as the most significant differences; but the impression was one of pragmatism without resignation. Little race bias was shown by any immigrants, but the non-whites were very critical of the implicit and hypocritical racialism of the British, who (it was claimed) did little or nothing to reduce the cultural, social and economic gaps between them and immigrants, and thereby increased the social distance and misunderstanding between the British and other people. The immigrants of all races perceived themselves as friendlier, more industrious, stronger, more honest and more direct than the British. The British, remarked one man from St Kitts, should learn 'the natural tolerance' of the coloured peoples:

'I don't think that whites have the same depth of feeling as we coloured. As a race, coloured have been subjected to all sorts of insults. Whites could acquire tolerance and patience from them.'

Experiences of discrimination were mentioned by almost all the coloured informants, and few had not suffered personally from an incident that shamed or angered them. Nearly 20% of the non-whites and 15% of the whites said that discrimination had become worse – only the immigrants born in the UK argued that there was less than formerly. Of the coloured informants 19% gave examples of how they had suffered discrimination in applying for a job, 11·5% complained about discrimination in the labour exchange, and 12·5% had had unpleasantness and embarrassment in shops or in obtaining services. Nearly 5% of the non-whites had had 'trouble' in obtaining a mortgage. On the contrary, of the whites only about 6% claimed to have had bad treatment at the labour exchange and less than 2% in any other field.

It is impossible not to sympathize with a Jamaican woman, who having cited several seemingly well-authenticated incidents remarked:

'You can only complain if things happen to you, but what goes on affects everybody, not only me because of my colour. You don't remember things to make a statement on, but you remember that your heart had been hurt. . . .'

The conclusions that can be drawn from the many studies are as mixed as the complicated patterns of rejection and acceptance that immigrants – particularly non-whites – have to face. The first and second generation of immigrants have probably not yet found the psychological means to fight from *within* a society which in part rejects and in part accepts them; they have two equally distressing alternatives. One can Uncle Tom or one can reject the host society. It is increasingly obvious that the numbers of young non-white immigrants who are emotionally satisfied to Uncle Tom is diminishing, and a generation of disappointed, disillusioned, estranged and alienated young people is growing. It seems increasingly improbable that the older generation's solution of becoming culturally assimilated and yet able to fight on racial issues will attract many young people.

4. *Conclusion: How racialistic are the British? And why?*

The impression from a growing number of studies of areas and topics is that Britain's traditionally divisive social structure is moving with increasing rapidity towards a cultural and social pluralism, is which different groups meet and mingle with varying degrees of harmony and disharmony, and where socio-economic class distinctions are exacerbated by racial distinctions. In some aspects of life there will continue to be acute rivalry and hostility, in others indifference, and in yet others tolerance.

The scientific study of race attitudes in Britain began with a comparative study of prejudice in England and France, which found that a significantly higher proportion of French informants than English were prejudiced against Negroes (LaPiere, 1928). It was found that in France the upper classes were strikingly more prejudiced than the lower classes, and urban areas were more prejudiced than rural, which was explained by the tradition of labour conflicts in the seaports. But in general, the French were remarkably free from prejudice compared with Americans. LaPiere continued his investigations by comparing the French with the English, and found a much larger degree of prejudice among the English at all social levels (from 73% to 90%), compared with from 4% to 67%). Among the English he found that the lower classes were more prejudiced than the upper, but that the difference was slight. LaPiere found it difficult to account for these differences, but suggested that they must be embedded deeply in the cultural traditions of the two countries, and that a basic factor was the *nature* of contacts that Negroes had with the host populations. In England the Negroes' contacts were influenced by the colonial and imperial past, and by English insularity and mild (or severe, at times) xenophobia. In France, '*la mission civilisatrice*' disposed the French to assimilate or to accept Negroes as Frenchmen. In France and in France d'Outre-Mer, Africans learned to become Frenchmen. In Britain and in British-dominated territories they were taught to become subordinates, and the creation of an élite of tame, educated administrators from among the 'native' population was maintained at a very low level. Further, the values and traditions of French society were open and welcoming to Negroes of high social status; those of British society were closed and rejecting.[1]

In 1939, LaPiere's studies were followed up (Adinarayaniah, 1939, 1941) but needed little modification. French students were much less prejudiced than the general British public, and the general British public was much more prejudiced than British students. Overall, the French were still less prejudiced than the British eleven years earlier.

Tumin (1967) extended the earlier studies to measure the social distance between British and Americans, Germans, Jews and West Indians, and found clear evidence that the West Indians were consistently less acceptable than the other groups as sons-in-law and neighbours, but were slightly more acceptable than Germans as workmates. This finding was similar to Ruth Lande's that

'a "coloured man" was an anomalous creature whom the British did not know how to place, like a stowaway. The United Kingdom was seen as composed fundamentally of ancient settled populations, fairly inhospitable to penetration, by everyone unable to speak English and not born on the islands. . . . The British gamut of "foreigners" [ranged] from the entirely vulnerable Negro to the powerful American, and included even folk who lived just ten miles away.' (Lande, 1952, 1952a.)

Other studies in the 1960s confirm (in varying degrees) the prevalence of racialist prejudice and discriminatory practices in Britain. Most discouraging (but difficult to assess) is Hill (1965). More balanced, better documented and by no

[1] It is perhaps indicative of the British ambivalence to their race attitudes that there is no equivalent to *Les Français et le Racisme* (Maucorps *et al.*, 1965); the closest seems to be *The Working-Class Anti-Semite* (Robb, 1954). Maucorps's study is a cooperative effort of social scientists to investigate with modern methods of attitude and opinion polling, four facets of the problem of racialism: (1) the extent and importance of racialism to French people; (2) its forms and manifestations; (3) its causes (individual and social), for instance, the role of public events such as the creation of the State of Israel and the Algerian war of independence; (4) the struggle against racialism.

means encouraging is Daniel (1968). Responsible and suggestive is the *Sunday Times* poll (7 May 1967), which posed four questions to its 'representative quota sample':

1. 'How much discrimination do you think there is against coloured people in Britain?
2. 'Would you be for or against laws to ensure equal treatment for everyone in housing and jobs regardless of their race or colour?
3. 'Do you think it should be illegal to refuse a job to someone because of his race or colour?
4. 'Do you think it should be illegal to refuse to sell or rent someone a house because of his race or colour?'

Most people polled agreed that there was considerable discrimination against coloured people: 23% said 'a great deal' and 43% said 'quite a lot'; only 1% said 'none' and 29% said 'not very much'. The second question was aimed at 'getting a general measure of sympathy for extending the Race Relations Board's powers', and indirectly for indicating racial attitudes. In favour of laws to ensure equal treatment was a surprising 58%, against was 31%, and 10% did not know. The poll observes that support for legislation dropped, particularly among Conservative supporters, when the question was put more directly: that is, having a coloured person living or working next to the respondent. A small majority were in favour of legislation to make it illegal to refuse a job to someone because of his race or colour, but more Conservative supporters would not support such a law than favoured it, and Liberal supporters were more favourable than unfavourable than other political supporters. Only 45% agreed that it should be illegal to refuse to sell, or rent a house, and 10% were uncertain. Again the Liberal supporters were more favourable, and the most opposition was from Conservative supporters, 52% of whom would oppose such a law.

The poll found few differences in replies when responses were arranged by age, sex and occupational class, and suggested that the issue of 'colour' and the attitudes to discrimination cut across political loyalties.

Hill's attempt to answer the question 'How colour prejudiced is Britain?', although praiseworthy in its intentions, is flawed by his extravagant partisanship and by the impossibility of evaluating the accuracy of his investigations. However, he makes some interesting impressionistic observations about the relationships between whites and coloured people.

Hill 'found' that there was a 'hard core of severely prejudiced persons' whose attitudes were not affected by their contact with coloured people, but that within the impersonal relationship of employment, the unprejudiced had their favourable attitudes confirmed. In the working situation, the coloured immigrants had made a favourable impression. The strongest prejudice was found among men under twenty-five and those over sixty and lessened between those ages; but most findings are that younger people are usually *less* prejudiced than their elders. Hill found that there was an increase in the level of prejudice among the host community in the issue of having coloured neighbours, which, in the area of his enquiry, was a possibility. Of those who had had coloured neighbours, fewer were prejudiced against them than those who had not (42%–53%). There was more prejudice about having coloured neighbours than there was about having a coloured workmate, and again prejudice was highest among men over sixty. Among women the proportion who would not have a coloured neighbour rose steadily with age.

Hill investigated attitudes in two personal relationships: inviting a coloured person into one's home as a guest, and intermarriage. He found 'a definite correlation between personal acquaintance with coloured people and tolerant attitudes'. Of the sample, 12% had coloured personal friends, and all of them would have a coloured guest in their homes, whereas of those who claimed to have had no contact with coloured people, only 42% would admit them to their homes as guests, and slightly over 50% said that they would not. Prejudice rose steadily with age among women, those under twenty-five being tolerant, but among men the trend was the reverse, with a prejudice peak between twenty-six and forty.

'A staggeringly high proportion . . . were against intermarriage, although many offered reasons in mitigation of their attitude, such as "it's the children who suffer . . .".' Ninety-one per cent said they would disapprove of intermarriage, 7% said they would approve and 2% made no clear reply. Again it was found that 'the degree of personal acquaintance makes a considerable difference to attitude': one-third of those who had coloured personal friends would approve of intermarriage, compared with 4% among those without coloured friends. Women were slightly less prejudiced than men: women under twenty-five showing 'a marked degree of tolerance'.

The PEP Report on 'Racial Discrimination in England' (Daniel, 1968) finds that racial discrimination varies 'in extent from the massive to the substantial', in different aspects of employment, housing and the provisions of services, and concludes that

'the experiences of white immigrants, such as Hungarians and Cypriots, compared with black or brown immigrants, such as West Indians and Asians, leave no doubt that the major component in the discrimination is colour.'

The consequences of the cruder forms of discrimination and prejudice are too obvious to need repeating, but the graver consequences are subtly concealed:

'. . . awareness of discrimination, hostility and prejudice reinforces any tendency on the part of people to withdraw into their own close communities where they can insulate themselves against its effects. . . . In short it will mean that coloured people will, themselves, increasingly come to accept the inferior role that is allotted to them in society, until the gap between black and white . . . becomes so great that the main outlet for the talents of able coloured people is the leadership of revolt.'

In effect, England is moving towards the recreation of

'two nations; between whom there is no intercourse and no sympathy; who are as ignorant of each other's habits, thoughts, and feelings, as if they were dwellers in different zones, or inhabitants of different planets'.

But whereas Disraeli was thinking of the rich and the poor, in 1971 it is not extravagant to think similarly about the relations between coloured and white people.

A revealing difference between immigrants of different races is their sources of disappointment with life in Britain. Of the total sample of nearly 1,000, 35% referred to 'colour and racial prejudice in general' and to 'unfriendliness to foreigners'. But whereas only 10% of the Cypriots expressed these feelings, 26% of the Indians, 34% of the Pakistanis and 41% of the West Indians expressed them. Next frequently mentioned were employment difficulties. Of the total, 26% and of this nearly half were linked to prejudice or discrimination. Again the Cypriots were least affected, only 9%, and most were the West Indians, 32%. The Asians were midway. The third class was housing difficulties, of which 21% complained. Of the Cypriots only 6% mentioned housing difficulties, of the West Indians 33%, and surprisingly of the Pakistanis and Indians 7% and 10% respectively.

The reasons for believing that a colour bar exists are significantly different for the groups. Only 16% of the Cypriots blamed discrimination in employment, compared with 62% of the Pakistanis, 58% of the Indians and 43% of the West Indians. Only 14% of the Indians blamed discrimination in housing, compared with about 21% for the other three groups. Only 2% of the Cypriots blamed discrimination in shops, pubs and public places, compared with 14% of the Indians, and 22% each Pakistanis and West Indians. But more difficult to tolerate emotionally was the 'general hostility of the host community', as exemplified in prejudice and abuse, racial slogans and propaganda, awareness of race through the mass media, and the 'general atmosphere'. Even the Cypriots were aware of the general atmosphere of hostility to, and lack of sympathy with, coloured people and immigrants, and all groups were subject to a mass of humiliating experiences, which though each by itself might be shrugged away as trivial, were cumulatively hurtful, disturbing and a continual reminder of a hostility that could erupt violently. Daniel cites many examples, such as the following:

'Even in the buses they won't sit against you. They stand up or move away. They don't want to live near us and when we move in they move away. They don't speak to us.'

'Clerical jobs are never given to us. I was educated here and pased my 'O' levels but I am refused a job whenever I applied for a clerical job. All the white boys I knew at school have clerical jobs but I have to be a labourer.'

Most telling of Daniel's evidence is the meticulous technique of 'situation tests'. In these tests a comparable West Indian, Hungarian and English applicant applied for the same post, or accommodation, or motor insurance. The conclusion is inescapable: the West Indian was at a considerable disadvantage, the Hungarian at a lesser disadvantage, and the 'reasons' advanced for discrimination along colour and 'foreignness' lines were most frequently mythical and unreasonable.

In 1969 the Institute of Race Relations (Rose, 1969) commissioned a survey of attitudes to assess the extent of race prejudice in Britain among the white population and, on the basis of questionnaires, divided respondents into four groups: the tolerant who comprised 35%; the tolerant-inclined who comprised 38%; the prejudice-inclined who comprised 17%; and the prejudiced who comprised 10%. These surprising findings have, however, been criticized on methodological grounds: see, for example, Rowan, *New Society*, 14 August 1969; and Lawrence, *New Society*, 21 August 1969. In the revised edition (Deakin *et al.*, 1970) the data are reinterpreted and unfavourable racial attitudes were found to be more widespread. But all such findings depend greatly upon the definitions of the investigators, and the interpretations of the statements by the people interviewed or questioned.

The 'explanations for the rapid development of racialism in Britain are rather inconclusive and mercifully few, but the recent emphasis upon colour prejudice has encouraged discussion to neglect the earlier example of the rise and fall of organized anti-Semitism. This suggests a possible pattern that *might* be repeated with non-white immigrants, and might assist in dispelling the myth that in some mysterious fashion the British 'democratic' and equalitarian tradition will automatically mitigate racialism – a view that seems to be implied in much of Anthony Richmond's discussion of the 'colour problem', and that of liberally minded sociologists.[1]

[1] Richmond (1961) holds the Utopian view that 'when Europeans are finally persuaded that the social, economic and political advance of non-Europeans is not a threat but a necessary condition of the prosperity of Europeans and non-Europeans alike, colour prejudice will disappear'. But the question remains unanswered: how much economic advance can remain compatible with prejudice and discrimination? The examples of South

The dangers of racialism cannot be assessed without some examination of the history of the fascist movements in Britain. A lucid analysis of anti-Semitism (Mandle, 1968), based upon an intensive examination of the documentary evidence, found three main reasons why anti-Semitism in the thirties declined startlingly after a dizzy rise:

'. . . the campaign failed first . . . because the essential context for success, a distressed or tension-ridden atmosphere was absent; in addition, efforts to create a crisis atmosphere and to heighten tension seem to have come up against a cultural obstacle. . . . A second reason . . . is to be found in the actions of the police and of the government. . . . The law did not abandon the streets to private armies as was done in Germany. A third reason is perhaps to be found in the nature of the anti-Semitism purveyed by the BUF. It was not of a high standard.'

Beyond this was the consistent and sometimes powerful and influential counter-attack both of Jewish organizations and individuals, and by those who disapproved of the BUF's destruction of law and order and 'civilized standards' in Britain. The dwindling and fissionary BUF has not been replaced up to now by any other party with influential anti-Semitic policies, and anti-Semitism seems to be confined to isolated individuals and organizations: more irritating than dangerous. The dissolution of a 'crisis-atmosphere', and positive efforts to combat social and economic inequality and to neutralize the semi-literate nature of most racialistic or (crypto-racialistic) propaganda, probably *might* now as in the 1930s begin to convert hostility into indifference, and indifference is not too far distant from toleration. But in 1971 it is still legal to publish such racialistic pseudo-scientific fantasies as Isherwood's *Racial Contours*, and a crisis atmosphere has been little discouraged by political and other leaders.

Most recent explanations of racialism in Britain have stressed (1) the impermeability of the British class-structure; (2) the homogeneity of British society and culture; (3) the increasing

---

Africa and of the deep South (see Genovese, 1966) make one distrustful of such naïve optimism.

dominance of middle-class values; (4) economic fears; and (5) the psychological vestiges of the stigmata of colonialist pride.

Analysts with as widely differing theoretical standpoints as Rose (1969) and Rex (1970) broadly agree that it is not physical appearance or even culture, language or religion that make immigrants socially visible. They are socially visible because their colour, culture, language or religion are associated with the low colonial status they had in their own countries. They come from a low status country to a society in which they will fit into industrial roles that are unwanted by the 'host' community and are of low status. Rex suggests that the immigrant also fits into the lowest ranks of the urban class system, and thus has a double low status: of belonging to low status within industry, and living in low status neighbourhoods in the cities. They are, therefore, vulnerable because they are socially visible and economically weak, and can all too easily become the classical scapegoat or pariah group.

Banton (1967), for example, argues that English society has been remarkably homogeneous culturally, with powerful tendencies to social uniformity within which class differences played a minor role. Even the provincial Englishmen had to conform to the national norms if he were to succeed outside his own region. And the national norm was – and increasingly is – the pattern of values of the middle classes. He draws attention to the skill with which Jewish immigrants have become as English as the English, and have been able to retain some of their Jewish cultural identity by becoming accepted as English in the most important areas of social life.

Further, the middle classes have become the dominant force in determining the overall pattern of cultural homogeneity. Wealth, schooling and education, accent, manners . . . have all taken a resolutely middle-class character, and the 'aristocracy' no less than the 'lower classes' aspire to middle-class membership and values.

One of the major considerations of middle-class cultural domination, Banton implies, is the ascription of people of lower status to a class of strangers, with unpredictable and undesirable (because not middle-class) behaviour. Coloured immigrants become the quintessential strangers.

Plausible though this argument is, it does not explain the

rapid growth of racialism during the past twenty years, or the middle-class resistance to racialism. It could be argued equally plausibly that one middle-class characteristic is its relative *permeability* to members of other classes, and its capacity to absorb them. A social class that could absorb (or capture) such unmiddle-class figures as Lloyd George, Ramsay Mac-Donald and Ernest Bevin seems highly accepting.

A curious variant of this argument is that the coloured immigrant is seen as a danger because he provides a contact *between* the classes:

'Into this [rigid] social structure arrives the West Indian and the coloured immigrant. . . . The West Indian speaks English with a middle-class accent, which is really hated by the working-classes . . . he is a living lie to all that was said of him – the black man. . . .

'The peculiar social structure in which the English people live goes down to living conditions. The classes live apart and never meet socially. In this scrupulously well-stratified society, there is no place for the African.' (Maxwell, 1965.)

Maxwell continues by arguing that the West Indians make the working class feel inferior, and the working classes have responded by attempting to 'push the West Indian and other coloured immigrants into the position vacated by the working-classes'. Anti-Semitism among the working classes (Robb, 1954), has also been attributed to similar economic and social rivalry.

The imperial-colonial relationship of the British towards the colonized, coloured peoples has possibly led to the development of a view that the British were (and still are despite all appearances to the contrary) more advanced morally and technically, and this has been reinforced by stereotypes of the undesirable qualities of coloured peoples, sometimes coupled with beliefs in their quasi-magical powers. Racialism is, according to this argument, the remnants of the arrogance of a colonial period, given a peculiar power by the insularity and imperviousness of the British social system and its severely hierarchical structure.

However, it is clear that other components must be taken into account: (1) the increasing number of immigrants in the post-1950s has revealed the squalid housing situation and the grossly inadequate social services. The fear of overcrowding and of straining the social services is partially rational. But the attack on immigrants has become a substitute for the radical planning of British society that can alone improve the quality of material living: (2) the economic instability of Britain has aroused long-established working-class fears about unemployment, and has stimulated the fear of losing jobs to 'cheap labour'; (3) cultural differences between the host and immigrant populations have not been decreased by the inept attempts at 'education for tolerance' by the mass media. All too often a non-white is portrayed in some unusual and glamorous role, and not in the same range of everyday roles as whites. A doctor of African appearance in a strip serial, or a Chinese nurse in 'Emergency Ward Ten,' or an idealistically attractive West Indian student in 'The L-shaped Room', are too easily isolated as 'different'. There is a need for non-white housewives, bus conductors or shop assistants, with whom there is some possibility of identifying and sympathizing. Coronation Street should have its Jamaican Ena Sharples – as it would have in real life; (4) political leadership has been slow, clumsy and faltering in combining reassurance, a firm disapproval of racialism, and clear and radical policies to alleviate social and economic distress and uncertainty; (5) legislation has been insufficiently used as an educative and norm-setting technique.

Chapter 5

A SOCIAL CASE-HISTORY:
SOUTHERN AFRICA

I. INTRODUCTION

In a remarkable historical and psychoanalytical exploration of anti-Semitism, Cohn (1967) warns against the unsophisticated error of assuming that the emotional roots of all varieties of race prejudice are the same. There are fundamental differences both in emotional content and in policy between the beliefs of a fanatical anti-Semite who strives for a world in which there would be no Jews, and those of a white supremacist who is content if Negroes exist solely to serve as inferior beings.

Similar errors can be made about the social and economic origins and functions of race relations, and the associated attitudes. It is a thoughtless polemic to equate the situation in 1971 in the UK with that in South Africa; it is more appropriate to trace analogies between the latter and the deep South of the USA. Nothing but confusion results from the statement of the Ghanaian delegate to the UN in 1967 who argued that *apartheid* in South Africa will inevitably lead to genocide, as Hitler's anti-Semitism led to mass murdering of Jews. The peculiar outcomes of economic and social stresses and conflicts, and the sometimes quite adventitious historical events that precipitate them, are as varied as the forms of the societies in which they exist.

However, an analysis of the South African situation is indirectly relevant to the understanding of the development of race relations in other parts of the world. In South Africa one sees in its most extreme form the development of a modern industrialized state based upon racial divisions, influenced by race and class conflicts. In one sense it is correct to say that the experience of South Africa is unique; the experience of any

117

society is unique. But the underlying tensions and conflicts and the consequent policies and practice in a modified form can be distinguished in other countries. South Africa's tragedy is a microcosm of the tragedy of a world divided into racial conflict. Moreover, South Africa demonstrates the intricate motivations of racism and a racist society, displaying both deeply irrational and often unconscious fears and anxieties, and the more conscious conflicts about power and privilege. The example of South Africa also demonstrates the inadequacy of purely social factors to understand the mass behaviour of a society, for even this society with its monopoly of military, economic and political power, is driven to rationalize and legitimize its position by the creation of myths and the rejection of any rational consideration of the ultimate untenability of its position. Segal (1967) writes that

> 'one need only consider the moral rot of white South Africa to see, in the world of the moment, the cumulative consequences of fear (for the loss of privilege and security) and hatred (for whoever may be suspected of menacing either) hideously magnified under the glass of race'.

White South Africa has collectively retreated, together with its material wealth, into a fantasy world in which threat, danger, chaos and insecurity have to be unceasingly combated. But every effort to contain or control the threatening world serves only to reinforce the fear that this threat exists. This is the paradox of the Dance of Death: the dancers dance frantically to escape Death, but in the end dance themselves into exhaustion – and death. South Africa demonstrates that once a nation embarks upon the determination to justify itself by an ideology of fear there is no escaping the irradiation of all that society's activities by fear.

This chapter illustrates further the view that psychological, social and historical factors must be integrated to explain race relations. It shows how race relations, although influenced by objective socio-economic conditions, are also influenced by irrational factors that impinge upon the conscious social determinants. Socio-economic forces set limits – wide or narrow – to the possibilities of choice, but it is men and women and their children who do the choosing. It is men and women who are afraid, angry, prejudiced; or who are hopeful, farsighted and tolerant.

The writer believes, for example, that the fear and horror of 'miscegenation' is quasi-magical. It is a belief that there is some quality about the possession of a whiter skin that is destroyed by contamination with darker skins. For example, in 1928 the *South African Medical Journal* published a major 'biosociological' survey of 'The Colour Problem', the main theme of which was 'to discover how far and in what manner the coloured and white communities may live side by side without becoming mutually destructive, and to what extent . . . the coloured community could ever be recognized as of eugenic value'. (*S.A. Medical Journal*, 1928, II, 324–32). Few scientists would now regard these problems as scientifically meaningful. No doubt some part of the fear of miscegenation is related to a determination to preserve the economic and status privileges of a caste. But the extra-ordinary lengths to which a society goes to maintain caste barriers, and the risks that are taken to break them, suggest that unconscious motives other than simple social and economic gain are involved.

II. THE PRESENT PATTERN OF RACE RELATIONS IN SOUTH AFRICA

Population:[1] South Africa, twice the area of France, if one excludes the vast and empty South West Africa, is relatively thinly populated. It has an average density of about 36 people per square mile, compared with the 567 of Britain. In mid-1966 the estimated size of the population was:

Whites	3,481,000
Coloureds	1,805,000
Asians	547,000
Africans	12,465,000
	18,298,000

The population is expected to increase considerably (by natural

[1] One of the explanations offered for the development of race relations in Southern Africa has been the disparity in numbers of Africans and non-Africans, and the scattered and vulnerable white populations.

increase rather than by massive immigration), and various estimates of the total population in the year 2,000 range from nearly 29 millions to over 31 millions. The natural increase rate of Africans is not published, but that for other groups is: Whites 13·6 per 1,000, Coloureds 30·3, and Asians 26·3; the infant death rate is also not published for the Africans, but for whites it is 29·2 per 1,000 live births, for Coloureds 136·1, and for Asians 56·1.

More important is the area distribution of the population, and here the most significant feature is the steady increase in urbanization of the Africans. The preliminary results of the 1960 census gave the following percentages for the population living in urban areas: African 30, Coloured 63, Asian 80 and White 80. About 44% of the total population is urbanized. Johannesburg has well over a million inhabitants, of whom about half are Africans; Cape Town is approaching a million, of whom nearly half are Coloured and a mere 10% are Africans; Durban is nearing three-quarters of a million, of whom about one-third are Africans and one-third are Indians; Pretoria is nearly half a million, of which almost half are Africans.

> The economist Horwood considers that the official figures '. . . reveal quite clearly that the urbanization rate of the African has outstripped that of any other race. Where, in 1911, there were approximately half a million Africans in the urban areas, the number had increased to some three million by 1960. Where, fifty years ago but one in every eight Africans resided in the Metropolitan areas, today three in every ten do so. During the last intercensal period (1951–1960) there was a bigger increase in the urban African population than in any similar period in the past. What is more, a sample survey reveals that 70% of urban Africans are industrialized workers who have never reverted to rural work.' (Horwood, 1962.)

Education. South Africa has different systems of education for its different race groups. The whites have better education in terms of money spent per head (approximately ten times that spent on African pupils), and in the quantity and quality of instruction. The Africans of all the non-white groups fall most seriously behind, and this is most plain in the higher levels of education. For example, Makerere University College in Uganda annually graduates almost three times as many medical practitioners as Natal University's segregated medical school. An even more striking comparison: in 1966 the tiny state of Guyana was founded with 160 doctors, 17 dental surgeons, 3 architects with ARIBA qualifications, 33 civil engineers, 20 electrical engineers, 14 mining engineers ... and 19 accountants and auditors with appropriate qualifications (*The Times*, London, 23 May 1966).

By comparison the record of South Africa is deplorable. Wealthy, populous, and with an education system over two hundred years old, annually fewer than 800 Africans matriculate, about 56,000 reach secondary school, and the cost of educating African pupils is about £6.10s per annum (R.13·82 in 1964–5). Not surprisingly, in 1964, of the 8,468 registered medical practitioners, only about 100 were Africans; about 15 graduate annually from the one medical school open to them. There are no African architects; only three Africans have qualified as engineers of any kind, and none has practised in South Africa in his speciality; there are no Africans with higher qualifications as accountants or auditors; there are no African dentists, and in 1964 the first African qualified as a pharmacist.[1]

In mid-1966 there were approximately 65,000 enrolments in South African universities and university colleges, of which about 2,900 were Africans, 3,000 were Asians and 1,290 were Coloureds. The Minister of Bantu Education stated in the House of Assembly on 11 February 1964 that since 1956 the following numbers of Africans had obtained university degrees: 1956 – 144; 1957 – 182; 1958 – 177; 1959 – 197; 1960 – 186; 1961 – 182; 1962 – 105 (Hansard, 4, col. 1122). These numbers are so small both in relation to the total number of Africans with skills and to the economic and technological needs of South Africa as to be almost without any significance. But they demonstrate that the system of separate development is not en-

---

[1] See Horrell, M., *A Survey of Race Relations in South Africa* (S.A. Inst. of Race Relations, Johannesburg), annual; Horrell, M., *A Decade of Bantu Education*, S.A.I.R.R., 1964; Hurwitz, N., *The Economics of Bantu Education in South Africa*, S.A.I.R.R., 1964; Kuper, L., *An African Bourgeoisie* (Yale U.P., 1965); Bloom, L., 'Education for Africans in South Africa', *Integrated Education*, 1965, III, 4–5, 89–94.

couraging the development of an educated and skilled class of Africans who might, conceivably, be able to 'develop' separately and equally.

It seems no exaggeration to state that for the overwhelming proportion of Africans, and a large proportion of Coloureds in South Africa, education ceases when the young person is still functionally illiterate, even though he is able to read and write simply in English and/or Afrikaans, and to understand simple orders in those languages.

The rationale has been clearly explained by Dr Verwoerd, in the debate in the House of Assembly on what was then known as 'Native Education':

> 'Native education should be controlled in such a way that it should be in accord with the policy of the state . . . Good racial relations cannot exist when the education is given under the control of people who create wrong expectations . . . Education must train and teach people in accordance with their opportunities in life, according to the sphere in which they live.' (Hansard, 1953, V. 10.)

In effect this means that African education is to maintain Africans so that they do not present a threat to the economic and social privilege of the whites. This is oddly reminiscent of the attitude toward working-class education of the early nineteenth century.

Legislation. The general pattern of a segmented South Africa is enforced by an elaborate system of laws that (1) classify the population by race and take measures to prevent the mingling of races; (2) limit the political and civil rights of non-whites; (3) enforce residential and territorial segregation of races; (4) reserve training and employment for the different races; (5) restrict educational and social amenities to different races.

1. *Race classification* has been law in South Africa since 1911, but only since the Population Registration Act of 1950 has it become both rigid in its administration and all-embracing in its scope. The broad principles are that the population must be classified by race as defined by both appearance and general acceptance and repute. Marriages between whites and non-whites are illicit and punishable by imprisonment or whipping.

There has been in South Africa about three centuries during which there has developed 'an increasingly morbid fear of miscegenation unparalleled in intensity' (Van den Berghe, 1960') coupled with a persisting breaking of the law. Among the white males who break the laws

'the prominence of the police and civil service (including the state railways) . . . is noteworthy. This fact lends indirect support to Lewin's contention that non-marital miscegenation is found more frequently among highly-prejudiced Europeans who treat non-whites as tools for the white man's convenience . . . . Policemen and railway workers come predominantly from the Afrikaner lower class among whom racial prejudice is deeply rooted.' (Van den Berghe, 1960.)

The classificatory laws are supplied with obsessive zeal, but despite the twenty years since the Population Registration Act became law, race classification is still arbitrary and uncertain. For example, up to 31 March 1964 nearly 4,000 objections to racial classification had been made, and the uncertainty continues.

2. *Political and civil rights* are narrowed by the laws that have (*inter alia*) largely abolished the political representation of non-whites by whites in Parliament, outlawed opposition by non-whites and restricted political association, gravely limited freedom of opinion and expression, and closely controlled the right to peaceful assembly and association.[1]

Political and civil rights are limited by a series of laws that claim to ensure public safety and to control undesirable activities. The major law is the Suppression of Communism Act (No. 44 of 1950), which makes illegal the furthering of any scheme or doctrine which aims at bringing about 'any political, industrial, social or economic change . . . by the promotion of disturbance or disorder, by unlawful acts or omissions . . .' or which aims at 'the encouragement of feelings of hostility

[1] See Brookes, E. H., and Macauley, J. B., *Civil Liberties in South Africa*, Cape Town, 1958, Oxford U.P.; International Commission of Jurists, 'South Africa and the Rule of Law', Geneva, 1960; Horrell, M., *'Legislation and Race Relations'*, S.A.I.R.R., Johannesburg, 1963.

between the European and non-European races' with a view to encouraging the success of any scheme or doctrine as mentioned.

Other laws have been used to proscribe non-white political organizations, including the African National Congress (founded in 1912), and to create a new crime of 'sabotage', defined widely enough to include a technical trespass. Further, the Criminal Law Amendment Act (No. 8, 1953) can impose fines, imprisonment, whipping or all three on persons convicted of any offence committed in support of a campaign to alter the law, and an Act of 1954 empowered the government to prohibit public gatherings in specified areas for specified times. There is further control of publications. The increasingly severe General Law Amendment Acts (from Act No. 39, 1961, onwards) empower the government to detain people incommunicado, and to set up local courts which have been used to speed the conviction and punishment of political 'offenders'.

The whole legal apparatus has been employed to maintain the existing system of race relations by making a lawful protest or objection by either non-whites or whites virtually impossible, except within the narrow racist context of South African political life.

3. *Residential and territorial segregation* is controlled by the various Group Areas Acts by which the ownership and occupation of land is set aside for a particular race. This has necessitated massive shifts of population, and communities have been moved who were settled in areas for generations. In Cape Town, for example, in 1964 the area of District Six was zoned for whites, despite its having been occupied for three centuries by a community of extraordinary closeness that included in 1964, 61,000 Coloureds and Malays, 800 whites and 600 Indians. All the towns and cities of South Africa have had determinations, but the largest forced movement has been that of Africans from the Western Cape which, if completed. would be of a quarter of a million people who would be sent back to the already grossly overcrowded 'reserves'. In the meantime, the removal creates a large population of semi-skilled and unskilled migrant labour with no permanent and assured

rights to live anywhere. One result has been that nearly 900 Africans are prosecuted monthly in Cape Town for being there illegally; and between 1959 and 1963 over 19,000 Africans had been ordered to leave the city areas. But this migration is not confined to Cape Town. In the Reef areas, during the first three months of 1965 alone over 11,000 men and women were 'endorsed out' (Horrell, 1964, 1965).

By various Bantu Laws Amendment Acts, the right of an African to reside in an urban area is nil, and the control over him by the local officers of the Department of Bantu Administration and Development is almost without limit.

4. *Employment.* Various laws, in particular the Native Labour (Settlement of Disputes) Acts, No. 48 of 1953, and the Industrial Conciliation Act, No. 28 of 1956, have the effect of making it impossible for unions to be registered that cater for both white and non-white members, and place African workers at considerable disadvantages. Trade unionists in South Africa have always been divided on the race issue, and the laws have strengthened those unions that support a segregationist policy, and effectively prevent the development of a non-racial trade union movement in which the non-white workers can play a full part. The main non-racial body, South African Congress of Trade Unions (SACTU) has been allied with the ANC and other members of the Political Congress Group, and the government has now banned, imprisoned or banished nearly all of its leaders, so there is no major African or Coloured or Indian union at liberty in South Africa.

By Act No. 41 of 1959, it is illegal for employers to collect trade union dues from Africans, and the government took wider powers to prohibit strikes in services and industries that it deems to be essential. By this device it has made strikes by non-white workers almost totally illegal, though the same effect has been achieved by ordering many prominent union leaders to resign under the provisions of the Suppression of Communism Act of 1950.

But the severest discriminatory policy is that of 'Job reservation'. In 1924, the coalition government introduced 'the civilized labour policy' by which on the railways and in the public services, non-whites were replaced by whites. This, and later legislation, has protected whites from non-white competition in many trades and industries, and has made it difficult, (or impossible) for Africans to obtain apprenticeships that would enable them to compete as equals with whites and Coloureds.[1]

Many industries and trades have been affected by job reservation determinations that restrict employment to whites, including the clothing industry, the building industry, the driving of heavy vehicles in certain areas on the Free State Goldfield, the transport system of Cape Town municipality, barmen in Durban and Pietermaritzburg, skilled work in the wholesale meat trade and the operation of elevators in certain large cities.

The white unions, however, have begun to find even the government to be perilously near radicalism, since despite job reservation there have been increasing examples of non-whites doing a skilled job (and earning unskilled wages) because there is no white man to do the job. In 1965, there was almost open revolt among white miners on the Reef when the government suggested that Africans were promoted to partially fill a shortage of 2,000 white workers. A rebel union of white miners was formed, and unbridled racialistic agitation and violence broke out. The government was forced to withdraw its proposals, and the mines continued as before to use non-white labour as unskilled or semi-skilled labour.

Five years later, despite the pressure from English and Afrikaans industrialists to amend the job reservation laws, and despite the growing realization of members of the government that these laws are economically harmful to the long-term development of the economy, no appreciable alteration has taken place. The miners in 1970 again uncompromisingly refused to train Africans for skilled jobs despite government pleas (that were modified by careful qualifications), and the miners were supported by the leader of the extreme right-wing breakaway from the governing party. (*The Times*, 15 October, 1970.)

[1] See Hutt, W. H., *The Economics of the Colour Bar*, London, 1964, André Deutsch; Doxey, G. V., *The Industrial Colour Bar in South Africa*, Cape Town, 1961. Oxford U.P.; Malherbe, E. G., *Educational Reéuirements for Economic Expansion*, S.A.I.R.R., Johannesburg, ref.: RR 5/1965.

5. *Social amenities*, even in the more 'liberal' Cape Town area, have long been reserved for different races, and there has been slight social mixing of the races. But from the early 1950s the government launched a consistent programme of compelling rigid segregation in social activities. A major Act was the Reservation of Separate Amenities Acts, No. 49 of 1953, which empowered authorities to reserve public premises or vehicles for a particular race, and which made it a criminal offence to attempt to enter premises or vehicles from which one's race had been excluded. It further provided that no appeal could succeed on the grounds that the facilities provided were unequal. This Act was passed after demonstrations and massive passive resistance had temporarily succeeded in compelling the authorities to allow technical breaches of segregation. Some 8,000 arrests were made, and severe penalties imposed. (See Kuper, L., *Passive Resistance in South Africa*, New Haven, 1960, Yale University Press.)

As a result of the various laws there is now almost total segregation in the use and occupation of places of entertainment, cultural institutions, parks, gardens and zoos, public institutions from jails to post offices, in sporting bodies, scientific and professional organizations, welfare and charitable organizations; and in many – if not most – churches.

In sport too there is a steady movement towards complete segregation, and Africans are seriously affected by their being refused admittance to, or participation in, sports in which non-Africans are either participants or observers. In July 1967, for example, Africans were forbidden to fight in a mixed non-white boxing tournament in Durban, and were forbidden to attend the tournament. Promoter Nat Moodley said that this was the 'death of non-white professional boxing' (*Daily Despatch*, East London, 28 July 1967).

The rationale integrating this body of legislation is twofold: (1) the only way to avoid social conflict, the struggle for political power and the clash of cultures at 'different levels of sophistication', is to maximize the social and psychological distances between them; and (2) even apparently trivial contacts between members of different races meeting as equal blur the sense of racial distinction, and therefore ultimately erode race consciousness. A reason that is more difficult to reconcile with the mass of discriminatory laws is the belief that the only way to ensure – or at least to permit – the fair treatment of any race is to allow its autonomy to develop along its own lines, which necessitates preventing it from contamination by other races or cultures.

However, whatever be the rationale behind the legislation, it demands considerable intellectual dexterity to present even a prima facie case that the net result has *not* been to consolidate a society in which races are kept arbitrarily apart, gross inequalities exist, and hostility and suspicions between groups based upon intransigent racialism of the dominant whites are a major value.

III. THE BACKGROUND TO RACE RELATIONS

South Africa and Rhodesia still retain vestiges of their origins as frontier societies governed by a frontier mentality. Even in the late 1960s, attitudes linger that are reminiscent of the turbulent times of *trek*, and of wars with the Africans who fought to preserve their lands from invasion, their societies from ruin and their peoples from enslavement.

(a) *Rhodesia and Zambia.* Although missionaries and prospectors had been roaming East and Central Africa since the 1830s (or earlier), it was not until the 1880s that Cecil Rhodes, neatly combining chauvinism and cupidity, rapidly annexed what later became known as the Rhodesias. But even as late as 1895, a contemporary account by a supporter of Rhodes could write that the value of such a new country as Rhodesia 'has still to be proved' (Fitzpatrick, 1900).

In the Rhodesias, unlike in South Africa, there were comparatively few white settlers – company officials, colonial officers, missionaries and a few prospectors were not substantially augmented by a permanent body of white settlers until after World Wars I and II, when many former members of the British armed forces used their gratuities to establish farms and businesses. When copper mining began to flourish at the beginning of the century, artisans and semi-skilled workers also began to settle. But by 1919, Southern Rhodesia had barely 33,000 'Europeans', most of whom lived along the line of the railway, and there were rather more than (an estimated) three-quarters of a million Africans. The whites felt encapsulated and beleaguered, and this social isolation together with the tendency for families to settle rather than individuals discouraged concubinage. Further, from the earliest settlement in Rhodesia, the race attitudes of the whites were crude and violent (at the worst) and patronizing (at the mildest).

In 1923, the rule of the Chartered Company came to an end. The colony gained *de facto* autonomy and a steady policy of segregation and discrimination formalized in law what was common in practice. And a fear of Africans grew which

'was not simply [a consequence of] the threat of economic competition, or even of political infiltration; it was a combination of these factors together with the shadow of miscegenation and the presence of a vast mass of people across a culture gulf which seemed unbridgeable.' (Gray, 1960.)

The local factors that influenced race relations in Rhodesia can be summarized.

(1) *Population*. There has always been a small white settler population, and the former has been isolated within its own cultural and social resources, and has responded to its numerical weakness by well organized belligerence. They are mostly skilled blue-collar workers, able to earn high wages and enjoy a very high material standard of living, and have tended to be urban rather than rural. The African population, rapidly becoming detribalized, accepting urban values, desiring modern education and a participation in the government, has offered the whites a threat to their status and to their privileges.

(2) *Ecological*. Competition for land ownership and possession early became sharp, and as the result of direct expropriation and such devices as poll tax, Africans lost land and their right to free enjoyment of it. As industrialization has developed and as Africans have been squeezed off the land, so has the migration of Africans to the towns accelerated. There has been,

therefore, a politicization of Africans in the towns, added to their resentment at losing their land.[1]

(3) *Political Leadership.* It is an intriguing if insoluble question to consider how far the racial attitudes of Rhodesian whites have been influenced by the astonishing vigour of its succession of authoritarian leaders, from Rhodes to Huggins, Welensky, Winston Fields and Ian Smith. Also, of course, the political struggle in Rhodesia has taken place in a considerably less complicated social and economic system than the struggle in South Africa. Another insoluble problem is whether the colonial situation attracted authoritarian personalities who find a psychological reward in their domination over a subject race. The evidence is equivocal, but (as one might expect) the white settlers show generally authoritarian and repressive attitudes in many areas of their lives, and not alone in the area of race relations.[2] Rhodesia has never had leaders of the subtlety of Verwoerd, Smuts or General Hertzog, but has tended to attract men whose strength has been to maintain the frontier tradition even within a growing urban society.

(4) *Social Structure.* From the earliest times there was not in Rhodesia the same accommodation between Africans and settlers as there was in the Western Cape. There was neither 'miscegenation' nor the ambivalent closeness of slavery. There was never a 'coloured' population, which in the Cape served slightly to mitigate the harshness of attitudes of white towards nonwhites. Further, the settlers in the Rhodesias acquired an affluence that the earlier Boers in the Cape never had. There was a far narrower gap in culture and living standards between the whites and non-whites in the Cape than in the Rhodesias. It took time for an aristocracy of wealth to form in the Cape: it was formed early in the Rhodesias. Lastly, in the Rhodesias, although for convenience one describes the whites as 'settlers',

[1] See Woddis, J., *Africa – The Roots of Revolt* (1960, Lawrence and Wishart, London), for a well-documented and perceptive analysis of the socio-economic consequences of land-hunger in Africa.

[2] See Rogers and Frantz, *Racial Themes in Southern Rhodesia* (1962, Yale U.P.; and the detailed analysis of essays by white high school boys in Rhodesia by Holleman *et al.*, 1962.

they are a highly transient population, and possibly this feature of its social structure has encouraged race relations based upon relatively uncomplicated economic motives, with fewer of the pathological irrationalities of attitudes in South Africa.

In Zambia, race relations have always been less tense than further south, mainly because the white population has included many colonial civil servants and professional people, whose high standard of education, and social and geographical insulation tended towards attitudes that approximate to those of the middle-class English towards their servants. Only in the Copper Belt has there been persistent and bitter friction between whites and Africans. In this area there still are a large number of whites working as skilled and semi-skilled artisans and supervisors, earning eages and salaries considerably more than those of Africans. Economic rivalry has frequently led to intense racialism by the whites, spilling over from the work situation to social life, and even in 1971 there are bars and meeting-places in the Copper Belt much frequented by whites where few Africans would care to go alone.

More generally throughout Zambia, because of (1) the wide disparity between the education of whites and Zambians, (2) the income differences between races, and (3) the tendency of the few middle-class Zambians to retain a marked suspicion of whites and shyness in their company, the social lives of whites and Zambians are in two worlds that rarely touch, even within the 'multi-racial' university. The writer, for example, lived about eight miles from the centre of Lusaka, and had one African neighbour. Across the main road, at about a quarter of a mile, was an area of working-class and upper working-class homes, in which there was no white resident. It is still uncommon for Africans to visit whites, and the writer was conscious of his neighbours staring surreptitiously at his African visitors.

The underlying tensions in Zambia are 'tribal', exacerbated by a divergence of interests between the more and the less educated, and between the urban and rural-orientated. But these tensions have already much of the intensity of race attitudes. For example, in August 1967, at the Mulungushi conference of the ruling party, the voting for party executives (and thereby for members of the government) took tribalistic lines that President Kaunda attacked fiercely. Shortly afterwards an anonymous leaflet was circulated in Lusaka which accused the government of being dominated by the Bemba and of repressing the aspirations of other language groups. It asked if the ruling party's slogan – 'One Zambia–One Nation' – did not mean 'One Zambia–One Nation–One Tribe', and during 1968 political alignments became increasingly 'tribalistic' as groups jockeyed for political power and influence.

But the ruling party, with unimpeachable integrity, although with pardonable – if unquenchable – naïvety, has adopted a policy called Zambian Humanism (a mild form of Christian socialism) in which sectionalism of a tribal or a racial variety is trenchantly condenmned.

(b) *South Africa.* In South Africa fatalistic attitudes towards the possibility of harmonious race relations are partially derived from the official myths of the development of race relations. The *locus classicus* of the official account is the Tomlinson Report on 'The Socio-Economic Development of the Bantu Areas',[1] which asserts (tautologically) that racial hostility in South Africa stems from 'strong racial feeling' and attributes this to six factors:

(1) The early clash between Christian and non-Christian religions, which favoured the solidarity of Europeans. As the early colonists had a strongly Calvinistic faith, they easily accepted themselves as the elect and the Africans as subordinate, tainted and in need of salvation and redemption.

(2) 'The differences in civilisation'. These are exaggerated by the Report. In the early days of colonization in the Cape there was little to choose between the Africans and the Dutch in material terms, and in broadly cultural terms a comparison is impossible and capricious.

(3) 'The racial, biological differences', it is argued, 'led to a feeling of aloofness and physical aversion' by the Europeans towards the Africans. The Report does not, however, explain the ease with which the practice of 'miscegenation' developed.

(4) The differences in economic and social status: 'the insti-

[1] The official one-volume summary is in *South African Affairs*, 16 April 1956, Vol. 3, No. 8, pp. 1–80, which must be read together with Supplementary Fact Paper No. 506, January 1957.

tution of slavery strengthened the opinion that the non-European is in effect socially and economically subordinate to the European'.

(5) 'The combatant relationship' gave rise to an unshakable resolve on the part of the Europeans to maintain themselves.' The Report ignores the struggles of the Africans to defend their lands and their liberties against the invaders from Europe, which seem not to have resulted in racialism to a marked degree among Africans.

(6) The difference in numbers, which compelled the European to take measures 'to ensure his own survival as a member of a minority group'.

After some dubious history, the Report comes to the conclusion that

'the racial factor became the symbol of these differences and the struggle for self-preservation and survival. Recently also, the growing consciousness of the Europeans' position as members of a numerical minority, not only in South Africa, but also on the African continent, has led to a greater realization of the dangers threatening the continued existence of the Europeans as a separate entity.'

But the early colonial period was less simple than the official survey suggests.

(1) From the earliest times the settlers cohabited with the indigenous peoples, and the result has been that over the centuries the population that is officially classified as coloured has merged with the white population, and an estimate of 1935 already put the number of whites with some non-white ancestry as high as 25%.

(2) The contacts between the Dutch, English and Portuguese invaders and the indigenous peoples was not solely one of unceasing conflict or warfare. Robertson, in his classic study of the contacts between the Xhosa and the Europeans in the Cape, shows the high degree of economic contact, with the Europeans anxious to maintain good relations in order to have a supply of cheap labour. But by the mid-nineteenth century there was forced labour and recruitment of Africans, and the relations of Dutch and the Africans became feudal

and stratified. By the 1850s, in much of the Cape Colony there was a complicated agricultural economy, and Africans were ceasing to own land and were becoming wage-labourers. In 1864 diamond digging began, railways and coal-mining boomed from the mid-century, and by the 1880s the gold mines demanded considerable numbers of labourers. In fact, by 1911 'the Natives had been progressing so far that it was thought desirable to restrict their opportunities by a Mines and Works Act' (Robertson, 1934, 5).

But although the frontier and frontier traditions were by no means the only factors in the early development of South Africa, they did play a conspicuous part. Ian McCrone has described graphically the isolated and precarious society of the white settlers in the Great Trek period of the later eighteenth century. The basic problem that had to be answered by the settlers was, quite simply, 'Can we survive?'

By the end of the eighteenth century, after about a century of colonization, the relationships between the Dutch Government, the settlers and the indigenous inhabitants began to change.[1] The settlers pushed further inland and a new community was formed, unlike the more settled, more urban, slave-owning and corn and wine-farming community around the Cape Town. As the settlers pushed still further inland, their relations with the Hottentots (and other indigenous people) grew ever more violent, and the control of the overseas government and company more tenuous. In short, there was formed a community of 'Border ruffians' living in 'Frontier Slums', and by the late 1760s a situation of near-anarchy had developed similar to the wild days of the West of the USA a century ago.

Further, the God-fearing Calvinists, isolated from Europe, had to convince themselves of their *right* to survive. By the latter part of the nineteenth century there was a firm conviction by the Dutch settlers that their survival was a demonstration by God that they were the elect. There began to develop a

'charismatic mystique of a people with a special mission or destiny; and this kind of belief . . . – [involves] a hierarchi-

[1] See Walker, E. A., *The Great Trek*, London, 1934, A. & C. Black.

134

cal, authoritarian view of group interaction in which in-groups are rightly dominant, outgroups subordinate.' (MacCrone, 1961.)

The frontier tradition still lingers, though the Dutch are now Afrikaners, the country folk live in sophisticated cities like Johannesburg, and the wars with Hottentots and Africans are now only slightly softened into political struggle.

The term *swart gevaar*, the black peril, is still frequently used, and the writer has heard the present Premier himself address a *stryddag* (political rally, usually to commemorate some day of national celebration or disaster), in which he elaborately and apocalyptically compared the dangers of whites in present-day South Africa with the perilous position of over a century ago. During the campaign for the referendum on whether South Africa should become a Republic, Premier Verwoerd circu-lated a leaflet in the form of a letter to the electors – all whites – of which the penultimate two paragraphs were crude appeals to primitive fears more appropriate to the struggles of a cen-tury earlier.

Even the vision lives: any criticism of the basic belief in racial discrimination is regarded by Afrikaners as heresy, and prominent members of the Dutch Reformed Church have been prosecuted during the last few years by their congregations for heresy. In 1961, when Premier Verwoerd was shot at, a woman rushed at the press photographers and cried 'Don't you know that he is holy to us?' And Verwoerd himself, after the success of his campaign for a Republic, publicly declared that God was responsible for his Party's political victories, and that the Lord had given political wisdom to the Afrikaner people, whose duty it was to save Western civilization from a variety of perils including the coloured races and Communism.

IV. RACE RELATIONS AND RACE ATTITUDES IN SOUTH AFRICA

Mann (1969) has gathered an unexpectedly large number of studies by social scientists who have investigated the psycho-logical consequences of South Africa's race policies. Still the major source is the pioneer research of Ian MacCrone, which is an almost unique blend of experimental-psychological and social-historical techniques. MacCrone constructed two scales: (1) to measure the attitudes of whites towards Africans; and (2) to test the social distance of whites from non-whites. The former had thirty items assessing the favourability or unfavourability of attitudes towards Africans and included such items as 'I consider that the native is only fit to do the "dirty" work of the white community', and the contrasting 'I would rather see the white people lose their position in this country than to keep it at the expense of the native.' The latter scale was originally employed in Emory Bogardus's study of race relations in the USA, and measures the distance that an individual feels exists between his group and some other, by the degree of social intimacy that he will grant to a member of another group. There is, for example, closer intimacy in admitting an individual to 'close kinship by marriage' than in allowing someone to 'live and work in my country'. MacCrone devised a scale with five steps of increasingly close intimacy. Both tests and a test of fair-mindedness were administered to about 600 white university students who were classified as Jewish, English-speaking and Afrikaans-speaking, and they were increasingly intolerant of Africans in that order. Also in that order they were increasingly 'distant' from all non-whites. Curiously, however, no link was found between attitudes towards Africans and fair-mindedness. Where social distance is the social norm it is fair-minded to keep your distance. The social distance between groups was greatest where the contact would be most immediate, that is, it might be easier emotionally to accept a person as a fellow-citizen than as a brother-in-law or a class-mate, though it is often not difficult to suggest to people that the former leads steadily and stealthily to the latter.

Later investigations, for example, Pettigrew (1964), Lever (1968) and Bloom (1960, 1961), have confirmed that the Afrikaans whites are more consistently racialistic in their attitudes towards non-whites than the English whites. The Afrikaners cling tenaciously to their racial antipathies and their social distance as though it was neceesary to preserve the *volk* from defilement by alien races, and in many official statements there is still an undercurrent of paranoiac concern with salvation.

A social psychologist, Crijns (1959), suggests that the earlier race attitudes of the Afrikaners had the effect of welding the white together in defiance of an enemy who was both satanic and economically and politically dangerous. Further, the whites gradually conquered the Africans and Hottentots by superior techniques and social organization – assisted from time to time by a little treachery by the English administration. Technical superiority easily served to reinforce feelings of racial superiority, which were in turn based upon an élitist theology.

The hierarchical structure implicit in *apartheid* gives rise to a complex of psychological consequences to the people who suffer its pressures and conflicts.

(1) Cultural and social differences become misunderstandings, and misunderstandings are exacerbated and grow into conflict. On the other hand the possibility is missed of educating young people to feel that they belong to a society that has the considerable advantages of possessing a rich variety of culture.

In education even the content of syllabuses encourages antipathy and cultural suspicion, although it would be no more difficult to diminish conflict and encourage cohesion. In 1961, Professor Max Marwick drew attention to the 'inexcusable biases' of test books in social studies, including geography and history, which emphasized the government's point of view on the dangers of contacts between the races and encouraged a narrow and chauvinistic outlook. 'An Enquiry into History textbooks and syllabuses for Transvaal High Schools in 1960' found 427 divergences between the English and the Afrikaans versions of the same text. Race prejudice was severer in the Africaans text, though present in both, and centred about propagating the myth of 'the past savagery of Africans and their primitive tribalism'. The modern urbanization of Africans was as much ignored, as were misrepresented the early struggles between whites and Africans in what were wars for survival between invaders and owners of land (Johannesburg *Sunday Times*, 25 September 1960).[1]

In 1962, the government legislated the National Education

---

[1] See Auerbach (1966), who has published the results of an enquiry into history syllabuses and textbooks in high schools.

Advisory Council, the membership of which was entirely composed of supporters of governmental race policies. The aims of the Council followed Article 11 of a Draft Constitution for the Republic of South Africa, published in Dr Verwoerd's *Die Transvaaler* in 1942, and never repudiated by the National Party. Most of Article 11 is concerned with the policy to govern education, and includes the statement that

'the attitudes of whites over non-whites is being regulated in the spirit of Christian guardianship, the former over the latter. The principles of no mixing of blood and of segregation must be maintained as of fundamental importance for the future existence of a white civilization in the Republic of South Africa.'

In 1948 the Institute for Christian National Education was even more specific in a pamphlet that recommended that

'Native education should be based on principles of trusteeship, non-equality, and segregation; its aim should be to inculcate the white man's view of life, especially that of the Boer nation, which is the senior trustee.'

These aims appear to have been carried out explicitly and implicitly by the present government since it assumed office in 1948.

(2) Racial attitudes are reinforced by class attitudes in segregated schools like those of South Africa. The white child is taught by the example of his everyday life that he is superior to the black child and different from him. No white child ever has an African teacher nor an African school-mate whom he might join in the university or technical college. His schooling, by its very segregation, serves to suggest that he is a member of a master race, because in the school (as in everyday life) he only sees Africans as servants, cleaners or menials. The writer recalls waiting for a bus outside the University of Natal's medical school for non-white students, and overhearing a sceptical group of white teenagers from the Afrikaans medium high school debating whether or not the 'baboons' really studied there to become doctors.

(3) Educational segregation prevents a child effectively from learning to tolerate and understand the ways of another

group with different culture. Stereotypes are neither softened nor dissipated, and small opportunity exists to learn to everyday living and working together that within the unit of the nation a diversity of culture is desirable, welcome and exciting.

(4) A more pervasive consequence of segregated and inferior education (discussed at greater length later), is that it depresses the young person's level of aspiration. There is little incentive to succeed if the rewards for striving are meagre and capricious. Moreover, the generally low level of achievement encourages the myth of non-white inferiority that is built into the society, and may ultimately become a part of the ethos of the minority group as of the ruling group.[1]

v. CONCLUSION

The broad lines of the race policies of South Africa suggest the probable consequences of intensifying the 'milder' race policies of other societies. Their basis is now economic and status rivalry – though they originated in the peculiar conditions of the Frontier Period – but much of the 'small apartheid' has no function other than the irrational psychological one of maintaining an artificial physical separation.

It is impossible not to be reminded of the ambivalence of the neurotic *délire de toucher*. The more the neurotic shamefully desires some satisfaction, the more he creates complicated barriers between it and himself. He hates all the more vigorously and pervasively in order to control his unconscious love. Whites in South Africa are continually discussing the behaviour of the non-whites, and forever seek to define more clearly the differences between themselves and the non-whites. They affect to despise non-whites, but search ceaselessly for the reassurance that they, the whites, are both deservedly and, in fact, superior and dominant.

The strongly emotional ambivalence of simultaneously craving and refusing contact is often almost morbid. The intimacy of physical aggression has a scarcely concealed sexual motivation. The fear of 'miscegenation' cannot be divorced from powerful, unconscious temptations against which religious

[1] See, for example, Rosen, B. C., 'Race, Ethnicity and the Achievement Syndrome', *Amer. Sociol. Rev.*, 1959, **24,** 47–60; Horowitz, I. L., *Three Worlds of Development*, New York, 1966, Oxford U.P.

and political leaders unavailingly warn. The non-white domestic worker is in close, even intimate, contact daily with the employer, and although the worker may be socially invisible and politically negligible, he or she is a constant reminder of the attraction to whites and non-whites for the creation of the coloured people. The very social structure of South Africa dramatizes the paradox that it is impossible to escape from contact with those upon whom one depends. The relationship of dependence often is deeply tinged with fear and resentment. If it were emotionally possible to achieve the separation between the races that the governing ideology advocates, there would be little need for the elaborate geographical and legal barriers between the races, which are defined and redefined with the meticulous and chilly fervour of a compulsive neurotic. The less emotionally viable that segregation grows in an economically integrated society, the more barriers are built, and the more that society reminds itself of its failure to control its denied desires for communication and contact.

Less directly observable, in South Africa as in the USA or other societies in which segregation is increasingly enforced by violence, is that the society steadily develops resistances against sympathetic contacts between the peoples. There grows a more and more powerful 'taboo on tenderness' (Suttie, 1938). This is a defiance mechanism of the personality, in which the dependence of one person upon another is denied. If one is to be cruel without conscience, one must be convinced that it is immoral to be kind, to be tender, to accept that one may depend upon another. The increasing reliance upon authoritarian methods in South Africa, the USA (and elsewhere), sometimes overtly violent and sometimes implicitly, prevents the dominating groups from communicating with the dominated. A non-violent understanding of each other's needs, fears and anxieties grows increasingly improbable, and the assumption of a common humanity becomes more difficult to advocate persuasively to the dominating groups, whose frequent justification of violence suggests that there is, frequently, an unconscious sense of guilt and anxiety about the denial of human qualities to the dominated groups.

Chapter 6

SOCIAL PSYCHOLOGY
AND THE FUTURE OF
RACE RELATIONS

I. COSTS AND DISTORTIONS OF RACIALISM

The true costs of discrimination and prejudice are both moral and psychological, and are in terms of unquantifiable, often concealed, but nevertheless real values, damaging both to the quality of society and its members.

One example suffices. During the three years 1965–7 in the USA, rioting and racialism cost the deaths of 130 citizens and the injury of over 3,600. Nearly 29,000 arrests were made, and the estimated damage to property and the economic loss was about $714 millions. This period included major riots at Watts, Newark and Detroit. After the murder of Martin Luther King in April 1968, rioting and looting broke out across the USA from Washington DC to Oakland, California; from Denver to Talahassee; and in Washington DC alone more than 20 people were killed.

The intangible, concealed costs were the civic disruption and insecurity, the hardening of misunderstanding between whites and non-whites and the cutting short of social and political dialogue. The encouraging of a tough frontier philosophy of attempting to suppress social distress with violence is matched by a counter-philosophy that only violence will bring about social improvements. When the expression of social distress is effectively suppressed, the processes of estrangement and rebellious despair may be hastened.

The calculable costs of law enforcement are considerable, growing and purely destructive. In Los Angeles, for example, the police have experimented with a giant troop-carrier of 20 tons carrying hoses, a smoke-screen producer, tear-gas launchers, and a 0·30 calibre machine-gun. The Detroit police have claimed eight armoured troop-carriers, and Cleveland, Ohio, is deciding in helicopters. Money spent on armaments cannot be also spent upon improving the quality of life.

Economic costs and losses, although assessable, are arbitrary and meaningless in moral terms. The damage done to the fragile bonds of society is enduring, pervasive and possibly irreversible. An indirect economic cost is the wastage – psychological and social – of talents and skills that are atrophying, unexplored and unemployed, and are summarized in the statistics that the teenage unemployment rate for Negro youth is nearly 26%, and of Negro unemployment in the one hundred largest cities is nearly 7% – far higher figures than for the white population.

Pettigrew (1964) has shown that if the acquisition of skills of non-whites in the USA continues at the 1950–60 rates, clerical workers would get proportional representation in 1992, skilled workers in 2005, professionals by 2017, sales workers in 2114, business managers and proprietors in 2730. This implies that even the brightest and most ambitious non-white child cannot realistically look forward to professional or vocational equality with a white child. The non-white child has to overcome a powerful social inertia if he is to rise above the depressive effects of low status and negligible opportunities. It is harder, and more discouraging, for a non-white child to strive for excellence because the rewards are far away and almost unreachable, and the models almost non-existent. The inaccessibility and irrelevance of rewards leads to a lack of interest in education, which in turn reinforces the lack of incentives to rise above a low status.

The explanation of Pettigrew's observation is outlined in the US Civil Rights Commission Report, 1967: segregated education facilities are 'inherently unequal'. In the deep South only 3·2% of all Negro children in Mississippi, 3·5% in Louisiana, and 6% in South Carolina (for example) attended schools with white children. Indeed, the vast majority of Negroes who entered first grade in 1955 completed their high in 1967 without ever having attended a class with a white student. Not only was this another obstacle to *psychological* integration, but there is a large body of evidence that suggests that school systems are improved when they are desegregated, because of the efforts that then have to be made to improve the total school system rather than its white segment (Hansen, 1960, 1963). More generally, Negro college attendance was proportionally about 50% that of whites. In Washington DC, for example, until the school board was restrained in mid-1967, the education of white pupils cost $100 more per head than did that of Negro pupils. At school the Negro drop-outs rate is 60% higher than that of whites, and by the twelfth grade the average reading-level of Negro pupils is about three years behind that of white.

The education of the 'disadvantaged' is in content, style and values inadequate for remedying the child's overall disabilities, let alone educating him to take his place as an equal in an integrated society.

The 'disadvantaged' child becomes the disadvantaged adult whose economic and social contribution to his society is less than society can afford and his personality can tolerate.

'In general, the environmental press of the American colour-caste system tends to develop conceptions of self in Negro children and youth which result in defeated behaviour, as far as academic and political development are concerned.' (Kvaraceus, 1965.)

Further, the disadvantaged child lives amidst a clash of cultures and values: those of the low status group to which he belongs, and those of the middle classes which dominate the larger society. Clarke draws a parallel between the situation of immigrants a few generations ago in the USA, and that of the Negro now, but the Negro has the added burden of the socially-defined inferiorities of his race to handicap him more than his white immigrant predecessors.

Inadequate language skill is a permanently damaging disadvantage of low-status children in their inferior schools. The low-status child uses language that is sufficiently precise and flexible for most simple purposes of communication, but is inadequate and unsuitable for the increasingly elaborate, abstract and subtle needs of communication in higher education and in the skilled and professional occupations. The equipment for learning in a modern society is largely linguistic, and if the equipment is deficient then the content of that which is learned, and the ability to learn, will be correspondingly limited (see, for example, Bernstein, 1958, 1962, 1962a).

John and Goldstein (1964) investigated the way that children develop and test the meaning and manipulation of words by conversation and word-play with verbally more mature people. They cited evidence to show that in low-income Negro homes there was less verbal interaction of children with adults than in high-income homes, and that the *quality* of the communication in the poorer homes was inferior. Put generally, although lower-class children – both Negro and non-Negro – have ample opportunity to learn simple names and direct verbs, they have less opportunity for 'active dialogue' and for using language more flexibly. Therefore the disadvantaged child learns in an inferior style in a school that is probably itself staffed largely by teachers who have difficulties in communicating.

The writer, while teaching at the University of Zambia, found a similar difficulty among students whose pre-university education and family background was culturally impoverished. When the University of Zambia was opened in 1966, it was compelled for political and social reasons to admit entrants many of whom had grossly inadequate English-language skills and whose ability to deal with some conceptual and abstract material had consequently suffered. The performance of students therefore failed frequently to correspond with potential ability (as indicated by non-language-bound tests). The University is now experimenting with English language courses similar in aim to the 'Head Start' programme in the USA.

Psychologically, the most pervasive, intangible yet irreparable damage caused by membership of a lower-status group is the difficulty the individual experiences in establishing satisfying anchoring-points for his developing personality. Individuals identify themselves with groups: the relationships of these groups with other groups, their standards and their values enable the individual to evaluate his worth. The prevalence of maladjustment among many Negroes is less dramatic than the clinical picture presented earlier, but is possibly more disabling. The psychological malaise of many Negroes is founded upon their social status, not upon their individual pathology. They have social selves that suffer from carrying an image of low status, low aspirations, conflicting perspectives. The seepage of motivational energy and the lack of confidence that are inseparable from growing up in a society in which the individual belongs to a group that the wider society defines as apart, inferior and alien can be clearly demonstrated, and dare not be ignored (Shibutani, 1955; Shibutani and Kwan, 1965).

Evidence of identity conflict among even Negroes who are not apparently mentally disturbed is plentiful – and convincing.[1]

The development of identity conflict among 'normal' Negroes is well described by Derbyshire and Brody (1964) and Derbyshire (1966). Negroes in the USA are integrated into a society dominated by whites, and tend to introject the social attitudes of whites, including the white self-concept. The ideal personality type is that of the middle-class white Protestant. Nevertheless, despite his introjection of white values, the Negro remains a Negro within a hostile white society out of which he cannot contract and at the same time retain his mental stability. He is therefore born into, and lives throughout his life within, a society that employs double standards. His behaviour, values and idea of selfhood are continually fluctuating between conflicting, irreconcilable, and tempting loyalties and their consequent behaviour patterns. The Negro wants to be a Negro. But he also wants to be white. Society permits him to be neither, and his sense of identity is unstable and unrewarding. The normal Negro has little opportunity to identify himself unambiguously with any definite reference group of status in the wider society, and he therefore tends to have an unrealistic and distorted perception of the groups that matter to him. Boundaries between significant social groups are poorly defined, his membership and loyalty fluctuating. For example, an Uncle Tom is not necessarily a 'traitor' to his race any more than is a *kaf-*

---

[1] See, for example, Davis, M., 'Results of Personality Tests given to Negroes in the Northern and Southern US and in Halifax, Canada', 1964, *Phylon*, **25**, 4, 362–9; Gaier, E. T. and Wambach, H. S., 'Self-evaluation of personality assets and liabilities of Southern White and Negro students', *J. Soc. Psychol.*, 1960, **51**, 135–43; Karon, B. P., *The Negro Personality*, Springer, New York, 1958; Lefcourt, H. M. and Ladwig, G. W., 'Alienation in Negro and White reformatory inmates', *J. Soc. Psychol.*, 1966, **68**, 153–7.

fir-boetie or a 'nigger-lover'. A man can have only a frail and marginal feeling for his own group, may even feel alien to it, and may have a deeper empathy at some times for another. He may experience such severe conflict that his personality fails to become stable and integrated. Vontress (1966) observes that the Negro is subject to a peculiarly sinister stress: he is unconsciously conditioned by an anti-Negro society to hate Negroes, and therefore to hate and to despise himself. Self-hatred is the major component of the Negro personality, and much Negro aggression – both group and individual – is a result of a desparate effort to escape from the feeble self by making a masculine protest.[1] This view is supported in the analysis of Gregor (1965), who has attempted to trace the social origins of aggressive attitudes and conduct disorders in Negroes. He too believes that the Negro is compelled by a discriminatory society to reject his *own* group, and he therefore fails to develop a strong ego that can keep in check any tendencies towards aggression.

But it is not only the people discriminated against whose personalities suffer as a result of racism. Baldwin in *Fire Next Time* describes how a society which incorporates racist attitudes against one section of its people inevitably becomes insensitive and callous towards the welfare of all. The dominant group can only maintain its psychological equilibrium in a society that is cold, loveless and rejecting. And Baldwin asked whether it is psychologically meaningful for blacks to demand integration into a sick society that is built upon inhuman values. Once one denies human qualities to one section of the people, there is no way of preventing this denial to ever-increasing classes.

Indirect confirmation of this underlying struggle to find a satisfying identity is provided by the many millennarian sects among oppressed groups, which are either openly political like the 'Black Muslims' or have both religious and politi-

---

[1] It was argued earlier that *the* Negro personality is as mythical as *the* character of any large and heterogeneous group. One individual *will* differ from another! But in so far as there are uniform patterns of significant social learning that are imposed upon members of a group, broadly similar personalities may result, which may – or may not – display pathological qualities.

cal functions and ideals, like many African sects in South and Central Africa.

Lanternari (1963), in his study of modern messianic sects, writes of religious movements in Africa:

'. . . By making a display of their religious independence, the people strive to fight the racial segration, forced acculturation, or destruction of tribal life imposed by both the missionaries and by the colonial administration.'

In a repressive society like South Africa, where political opposition is perilous, there is a strong inducement to retreat into a pseudo-world in which frustrated social and political activity can take place free from the danger involved in direct political activity. It may not be feasible to directly confront the power of the state, but it may be feasible to defy it by retreating into another world in which the pain of oppression is mitigated by the certain knowledge of ultimate, God-given autonomy. Even in the far milder atmosphere of Zambia, there emerged in the early 1960s Alice Lenshina's Lumpa and a section of the international Watchtower movement, both of which sought exemption from many social and political obligations and attempted to flee into pseudo-societies based upon religious-political doctrines. Both are mainly composed of members of minor language-tribal groups with unrealistic secessionist aims and a feeling that the Zambian Government is both rejecting and repressive.

Sundkler (1961), in his brilliant study of *Bantu Prophets in South Africa*, vividly evokes the mass excitement of the Xhosa more than a century ago, among whom appeared a prophetess whose apocalyptic expectations of the immediate departure of the whites from Africa caused the mass slaughter of cattle and therefore acute and lasting economic and social disaster. Sundkler finds it difficult – often impossible – to distinguish the religious elements in African sects from a quasi-political protest and, more deeply, a means of offering oppressed individuals a meaningful status, security and hope.[1] But a negative

[1] An admirable analysis of the ideology of social-religious movements is the symposium edited by Bryan R. Wilson, *Patterns of Sectarianism*, Heinemann, 1967.

and injurious consequence of this socialized flight into unreality is the loss to the wider society of the political energy and the abilities of minority leaders. No society has such a surfeit of political and social wisdom that it can afford to drive into a millennarian wilderness those who may include some of its more independent and lively people. Moreover, no society can lightly accept the waste and weakness, and the dangers of violence in the disengagement and lack of concern of an unconsciously hostile estranged segment.

Among West Indian immigrants to the UK similar sects with quasi-psychotherapeutic and integrative effects are emerging.[1] Kiev has described how West Indian Pentecostal churches in London have a valuable function for 'emotionally isolated immigrants', by offering them a temporary refuge from the rebuffs and discomfort of racial encounters. The members are offered an orderly view of the world with a happy goal in the future for the converted. They can attain grace, regardless of their socially inferior colour-definition. They are drawn into a cosy and exciting community which supports emotionally the lonely and the bewildered. Probably the fervour and excitement of the services act as a catharsis. Much repressed aggression can be released in the dramatic, vigorous and mildly aggressive activities of singing and celebrating.

But it is doubtful if these defences against disabling feelings of inferiority are any more durable than dreams. To retreat into a self-imposed ghetto may be the only psychological defence against the unbearable pain of the abrasions of hostile social contacts, but it is dangerously easy for this self-defensiveness to merge into a state that is close to paranoia. It can become a facile response to *any* frustration or anxiety-provoking situation to feel that one's race, nationality or even religion was responsible for the situation, and that one's own behaviour was irrelevant. Threat may be experienced and exaggerated where it may have been minor or even non-existent. This retreat tends, moreover, to be cumulative, which effectively prevents communication with other groups. This in turn encourages uncertainty about the meaning and motives of the behaviour of other groups, because only with contact can come understanding. There thus develops a spiral in which lack of

[1] See, for example, Gordon, 1965; Hashmi, 1966; Kiev, 1964.

contact exacerbates fear, anxiety and a sense of threat, and this inhibits contact. . . .

II. LAW, VALUES AND HUMAN BEHAVIOUR

Any social psychologist who proceeds beyond description and analysis towards even the most timorous and guarded attempt at prescription in terms of learning techniques for encouraging prejudiced citizens in a less prejudiced society cannot escape making among his recommendations some that may be translated into law. The influence of law in changing behaviour and attitudes is therefore often put in question. The psychologist is reluctant to join battle with those who argue law cannot change attitudes, or that law cannot enforce morality as effectively as education. Law, like all social institutions, is an elaboration of individual patterns of habit and has been learned through the various agencies of education in the society. Even though we are uncertain as to the precise mechanisms of learning normative behaviour, there is no doubt that within the school, the family and other proto-societies are learnt the rudiments of lawful behaviour, in similar ways to our learning language or other social behaviour.

There is no psychological support for *laissez-faire* objections to anti-discrimination legislation, and such objections, surely as irresponsible as were objections to factory legislation in the nineteenth century, are no less based upon a false psychology of an isolated self, unamenable to social influence and impervious to the possibility of change.

Indeed, law plays an influential part in creating change because:

'The popular notion that law reflects the *mores* is, as countless historical examples show, often the reverse of the truth. Law helps make the *mores*.' (Hutchins, 1961.)

Of course, no law will be effective unless it has the support – tacit or overt – of a substantial number of the people to whom it applies. But this number need not be a majority. Indeed, as social welfare legislation demonstrates, the public mood has often changed and *mores* have been modified once laws have been introduced. Slavery, child labour and hideous factory conditions are only three among the many undesirable *mores* that legislation abolished successfully, despite the tenacity of vested interests and of the pusillanimous, who argued vehemently that the law could not change society for the better. Herbert Spencer in his *The Study of Sociology* was the spokesman for those who gloomily attacked the 'vague faith in the immediate possibility of something much better than now exists – a tacit assumption that, even with men as they are, public affairs might be much better managed'. Fortunately for the slaves, the child-labourers and workers in wretched factories and mines, legislators persisted in not waiting patiently for men to be different.

Law *can* – and frequently does – create morality, but its power is less in its direct attempts by enforcement than in its support of other more educational forces. Anti-discrimination laws with heavy penalties are not designed to make racialists love their neighbours. But by discouraging openly racialistic behaviour, they make hating the neighbour less common, less socially disruptive, and possibly less 'respectable' – even in a sociologically uneducated society. Law does not much concern itself with the beliefs of the citizens – outside totalitarian states – though it is concerned with the social consequences of those beliefs. Moreover, the prestige and power of governments and law is often as powerful as custom, and can be highly influential on those whose views are not held tenaciously.

No law, for example, will make a coloured family welcome in a hostile housing estate, but if the family have an enforceable right to live on the estate, it is possible to prevent people from coercively depriving them of that right, and the possibility emerges – however difficult and delicate to make a reality – of both groups learning to live amicably together. Law *can* create social conditions in which human familiarity and contact can be fostered.

Law, in other words, provides the social foundation for the changing of group attitudes by creating or clarifying rights, and by establishing the means to protect or to enforce them. It can go further: law can sometimes accelerate change, as seems to have happened in the USA after the decision of the Supreme Court in 1954, which destroyed the old doctrine that facilities should be 'separate but equal', and ruled that equality before the law was an enforceable constitutional right.

Allport, in his *Psychology of Prejudice*, answers the question 'Does legislation affect prejudice?' with a carefully qualified affirmative. He concludes:

'(1) Legislation quickly creates new folkways; (2) When the initial work [of education] has been done, then the legislation in turn becomes educative. The masses of people do not become converts in advance; rather they are converted by the *fait accompli*: (3) People need and want their consciences bolstered by law, and this is nowhere more true than in the area of group relations; (4) While laws do not not prevent violations altogether, they certainly act as a restraint. They will deter whoever is deterable; (5) A final argument in favour of remedial legislation is its ability to break into vicious circles.'

A political scientist's consideration of recent American experience in enforcing anti-discrimination legislation supports Allport's cautiously optimistic conclusions, that if legislation is to be effective it must include the major areas of living, and the agencies enforcing it must have adequate powers. It is dangerous to rely too confidently on the educational influence of the law, and on expressions of sincerity (see Kushnick, 1967).

But a major problem is to estimate the intensity of discriminatory attitudes: some areas of living may be more susceptible to change than others. Equality might be resisted strongly in some matters and not in others. In the early 1940s Myrdal outlined 'the white man's rank order of discrimination', and compared it with the Negroes' own rank order; that is, the discrimination that he resists most, and that which he resists least. The white informants most strongly resisted (1) intermarriage and sexual intercourse between Negro men and white women; (2) social equality, and they supported the customs and the elaborate etiquette that serve as a denial of social equality, for example, the refusal to shake hands, to eat together . . . ; (3) integration in such public facilities as schools, churches and public transport; (4) political enfranchisement; (5) equality in access to, and treatment in, law courts, and equality in treatment by police and other public servants; (6) economic equality in, for example, purchasing land or housing, earning a living, obtaining credit.

On the other hand, Myrdal observed that the Negro least resisted the discrimination that the white man most strongly supported, and resented most the discrimination on the lowest level. This Myrdal agreed was because of the Negroes' most pressing needs – jobs and bread, even more than justice in the courts and the vote (see Myrdal, 1964).

Curiously, after a quarter of a century, it is the white man's *lowest* priority that has most effectively resisted change, and the demand for economic equality is the strongest Negro plea.

A recent reconsideration of Myrdal's findings considerably modifies them. Williams and Wienir (1967) found that a rank order for discrimination exists and is the same for white students in universities in North Carolina, Texas and Washington. The resistance to integration in the economic sphere is greater than resistance to legal, political and public facility integration, and the authors suggest that economic threat is a separate dimension. They also suggest that there is an overall decline in resistance to integration as one moves from the South to the North-west of the USA. But other surveys leave the picture less clear. In 1963, whereas 88% of the white informants would not object to working next to a Negro, 80% would not object to sitting next to a Negro at a lunch counter, and about 80% would not mind using the same 'rest room' as a Negro; nearly all *would* object to their own teenage daughter marrying a Negro, but only about 55% would mind a Negro family moving in next door or their child bringing home a Negro for supper. The survey concluded that the hard-core of prejudiced whites was about 20%, scattered throughout the country, and that the more intimate the possible contact between the races, the greater and more emotional the antipathy of whites.

In the same issue another survey explored the differences of opinion of whites and Negroes about civil rights and discrimination. On seven issues there was substantial – and surprising – agreement. Both agreed that Negroes are discriminated against, that Negroes' jobs are not equal to whites', that Negro education is inferior, that job integration is acceptable now, that Negroes should have access to all public facilities and services, that integrated education is acceptable and that Negro jobs will improve by the end of five years. There were only three areas of significant disagreement: only 3% of the Negroes thought that they were moving too fast, compared with 74% of the whites. Only 34% of the whites thought that the Negro 'rank and file' supported the Negro 'revolt' compared with 91% of the Negroes. Integrated housing was advocated by 78% of the Negroes compared with 42% of the whites.

The authors claimed that those whites who have had most social contact with Negroes consistently responded more favourably to the Negro cause and to Negroes personally, and the younger white Americans were significantly less prejudiced than their elders.

In conclusion: social values *do* change, and as part of the process of social change the attitudes of groups or individuals will often change correspondingly. But some individuals are more resistant to the influence of social change than others, and not all socio-economic and political change is equally effective in generating permanently modified attitudes.

Research strongly suggests that the reduction of prejudice and discrimination ideally depends upon three complementary approaches: (1) influencing the individual's personality and attitudes; (2) modifying the situations in which prejudice and discriminatory behaviour can be expressed; and (3) changing the values of the group which upholds discrimination and prejudice.

Earlier chapters of the book have described the genesis of racial attitudes from a narrowly individualistic point of view, and broader social factors were suggested rather than described elaborately. In considering the practical problems of encouraging attitude-change, it is above all necessary to demonstrate the widest range of techniques that are available to the social psychologist.

III. CHANGING THE PREJUDICED PERSON: OUR GROWING KNOWLEDGE OF THE MEANS

All people – prejudiced or not – support their attitudes and beliefs and justify their behaviour by an intricate pattern of devices that sometimes makes it difficult to dislodge them.

The *need* to maintain their beliefs often becomes an integral part of their personality structure, and this influences their perception and judgement of the world, so that they *perceive selectively* that which supports – or appears to support – their beliefs. Prejudiced people *feel* that the world is populated by dangerous and distasteful groups. They *distort* and misinterpret situations, and this provides them with spurious but (to them) convincing evidence. Therefore, education and other forms of persuasion may result in unexpected – and even extraordinary – behaviour contrary to the aims of the educator, as social psychologists have shown.

In one instructive and at the same time amusing experiment, prejudiced subjects were shown cartoons featuring 'Mr Biggott' and asked to interpret them. 'Biggott' was depicted as prudish and puritanical, unattractive and exaggeratedly racialistic. The cartoonist intended that the prejudiced person would see Mr Biggott as absurd and unpleasant and would, no doubt, modify these attitudes. However, this rarely happened: the cartoon would be misunderstood, the topic altered to some harmless subject, complicated motives were invented to support Mr Biggott's attitudes. In one cartoon Mr Biggott was in bed addressing his doctor: 'In case I should need a transfusion, doctor, I want to make certain I don't get anything but blue, sixth-generation American blood!' One subject reported was interpreting the cartoon as conveying the idea that if Mr Biggott was only a sixth-generation American he had no business to put on airs. Identification with Mr Biggott was effectively evaded, and the cartoon was diverted from arousing the viewers' insight into his racialism (Cooper and Jahoda, 1947).

There are, however, characteristics which are important in determining to what extent an individual's attitudes are modifiable.

(a) *Extremeness.* The more extreme an attitude the more difficult it will be to persuade someone to change it in a contrary direction. It is easier to persuade someone to change an attitude he holds with mild intensity.

(b) *Multiplicity.* Attitudes often occur in patterns that form a close-knit structure, so, for example, if a person has attitudes towards Jews that they are clannish, mercenary, cunning, energetic . . . he might be persuaded to relinquish one item yet retain the total attitude-pattern. In a study of a dispute about the fluoridation of a town's water supply, Mausner and Mausner (1955) found that the many anti-fluoridation arguments fell into three main 'themes': it is an experiment which may hold unknown dangers; fluorides are poisons; putting fluorides in public water is an invasion of individual rights and a step in the direction of socialized medicine. But these 'themes' were reinforced by an alarming medley of irrational allegations, varying from that fluoridation is part of a subtle conspiracy to . . . "paralyse, demoralize and destroy our great republic from within" by undermining us with a nerve poison in the water', to accusations of illness and death among fish and pets – even before any fluoride was put into the water, and most opponents of fluoridation wove together a tissue of contradictory beliefs. The disregard for consistency enabled the opponents of fluoridation to shift from one pseudo-argument to another without losing their pervasive attitude of suspicion and fear.

(c) *Inter-connectedness*. This is the extent to which attitudes are mutually supportive; the more closely linked they are, the more the arousal of one may stimulate the others. The difficulty in modifying the authoritarian personality arises partially from the intricately inter-connected pattern of outwardly unrelated attitudes and beliefs, an attack on one stimulating the emotionality and excitement of the entire pattern. On the other hand, attitudes that are isolated are more likely to be amenable to change.

(d) *Consonance* of attitudes means that an attitude that is broadly in agreement with others will be harder to alter than an attitude which is not. If you, the reader, support the British Labour Party, respect the Leader, support the policy of massive aid for urban areas and the Race Relations Act of 1968, to weaken your support of the Race Relations Act would be difficult because one positive attitude is reinforced by other positive attitudes. On the other hand, if despite being a Labour supporter in general you disapprove of the Labour Party's race policies, it would be easier to move you towards supporting them if your generally positive attitudes towards the Party, its leaders and its programme remain positive.

(e) *The individual's needs and goals.* The stronger the needs, the more strongly desired the goals, and the more of them that the prejudice serves, the more difficult it would be to alter the prejudice. An anti-Semitic attitude that is a major support of a cluster of needs and goals would be difficult to alter. In destroying the basis for the attitudes, the individual's personality might be seriously disturbed.

(f) *The centrality of the individual's values* will support his attitudes. His idea of what is good or bad, moral or immoral, may be held tenaciously. The more value-loaded, thus the more central and integral to the individual's personality are the attitudes, the more unlikely that his views will be shifted in a contrary direction.

There are individual differences in personality related to the readiness to change attitudes. The more intelligent individuals tend to be more able to appreciate an opposing argument, and the more educated individual can be more easily reached. On the other hand, a brighter and more educated individual might be better able to deploy argument, albeit of a spurious nature, to support his irrational prejudices and opinions. Janis *et al.* (1959) claim to have found a general personality characteristic of *persuadability*, and a study by Rubin (1967) suggests that this trait could be fostered. Rubin administered what was described as 'sensitivity training' and found that this increased the subjects' self-acceptance and their acceptance of others, as measured on a scale of 'human-heartedness'. Sensitivity training might therefore be a technique that could be used within the educational system indirectly to bring about reduction of ethnic prejudice by improving the individual's feelings about himself.

But the specific social and individual conditions that bring about attitude change are so many and so varied that considerably more research will have to be done before we can be more certain that our efforts will decrease and not increase prejudice. It should be some small comfort that industry and commerce have developed fairly sophisticated techniques for changing attitudes, although in areas of life often more trivial and less strongly emotionalized than prejudices.[1] Two major classes of variables that emerge in many studies are (1) the individual's general level of social adjustment and his mature ability to respond to changes in his environment, and (2) personality variables such as his aggressive needs and his attitudes towards other people, for example, his acceptance of other people.

Mussen (1950) attempted in a now basic study to test the relationship between personality and change in attitudes towards Negroes after intimate contact. His study was carried out at an inter-racial boys camp where Negro and white boys lived, ate, and played together, and where there was no racial segregation in any of the activities or facilities. Of the 106 boys in the camp, 28 became significantly less prejudiced against Negroes, but 27 boys became significantly more prejudiced. How did the groups differ?

'The children who increased in prejudice tended to be those who harboured more aggressive feelings and needs and had greater needs to defy authority. . . . They felt that they themselves were the victims of aggression, and that the people in the environment were not kind and helpful.'

On the other hand, those whose prejudice decreased

'. . . tended to have fewer aggressive needs, hence had less need to displace their aggression . . . They felt less aggressive press from the environment, far less fear of punishment and retaliation for the expression . . . and had a generally more favourable attitude towards others in the environment.'

Mussen found that although certain social factors in the organization of the camp were conducive to changes in the direction of less prejudice, some boys had a certain personality structure that made them 'susceptible' to change, and others were more impervious.

Other studies lend support to the proposition that even

[1] A lucid account of approaches to attitude change is E. E. Jones and H. B. Gerard: *Foundations of Social Psychology* (John Wiley, New York, 1967.) Also, McGuire, W. J., The nature of attitudes and attitude change in, Lindzey, G. and Aronson, E. *The Handbook of Social Psychology*, vol. III (Addison–Wesley, 1969).

race or group membership may be less powerful in determining prejudice or discrimination than the belief in important issues or the acceptance of an ideology. Even in South Africa there are whites whose belief in Communist or Christian doctrine serves to insulate them to some extent from the influence of the main flow of racialist ideology. One controversial study was that of Rokeach and Mezei (1966) who compared whites and blacks in the USA, whites who were high with those who were low in anti-black prejudice. They carried out their research in the State of Michigan where prejudices were less institutionalized than in other parts of the USA, but they made allowances for there being, therefore, less pressure from society to conform to racist beliefs. The authors concluded that racial attitudes are probably less important in determining prejudiced behaviour than what the individual believes about the other person or group, and if their beliefs can be shown to be congruent then attitudes are, correspondingly, modified. And most beliefs about race are subject to the social constraints and values of one's actual or reference-group.

One of the essentials of situations in which discrimination is practised and prejudice exists is, of course, that the society constrains people to believe that blacks and whites do have dissimilar beliefs, values and even personalities. Society makes it possible to treat people differently without necessarily hating them on an individual level, that is, face to face.

Can we expect that there is sufficient similarity between all prejudiced people to permit us to use the same tactics in attempting to change their attitudes?

Merton (1949) has usefully classified four types of people for whom different tactics would be appropriate:

1. *The unprejudiced non-discriminator*, who should lead in any effective campaign but whose strength is weakened by his tendency to indulge in meetings of the converted. The writer still recalls with some dismay and a little embarrassment the Liberal Party gatherings in South Africa in which worthy men and women addressed either other Liberals – or members of the political police. This type is in danger of overestimating the persuasiveness of the liberal approach, and may even encourage discrimination and prejudice because of his inability to contact

out-group members. Merton observes that this type 'essays a *private* solution to *social* problems'. The present writer believes that they too frequently confuse social, economic and psychological questions by employing moral arguments and hoping for moral conversions.

2. *The unprejudiced discriminator*, without having any deeply prejudiced attitudes, supports discriminatory practice if it is profitable or less trouble. Timidity, cupidity and expediency motivate him. Yet he has a sense of guilt, and he could frequently be reached if offered emotional and social rewards to abandon his discriminatory behaviour and to follow his beliefs. This type would refuse to employ Negroes because his customers might object, but supported by anti-discriminatory laws, he would be willing to employ them.

3. *The prejudiced non-discriminator*, or 'fair-weather liberal', is a conformist who discriminates until it is no longer expedient to do so. He is, for example, the prejudiced employer who refuses Negro employees until a fair employment law discourages him. Merton makes the distinction that 'whereas the timid bigot is under strain when he conforms to the creed, the timid liberal is under strain when he deviates'. The timid bigot can be inhibited from expressing his bigotry if he knows that it does not pay and that it is illegal. The timid liberal can be kept from discrimination by an appeal to his sense of values and by positive social support.

4. *The prejudiced discriminator* practises what he believes. He does not believe that discrimination is wrong, nor would he defend it on the grounds that it is expedient. He believes that the differences between races (or other social groups) are 'real', and that there is no alternative but to order society accordingly. Many prejudiced people with fundamentalist racial beliefs, such as some Afrikaners with strong theological backing for their racism, are of this intransigent type.

IV. PROBLEMS IN DESIGNING AN EDUCATIONAL PROGRAMME

A major difficulty in planning a programme to reduce prejudice is that a different appeal is appropriate for each type of prejudiced person, but the types are not equally distributed in all societies or all social classes. MacCrone (1937), Pettigrew (1958) and Van den Berghe (1965) suggest that the racial attitude of South African whites is largely composed of the 'prejudiced non-discriminator', who discriminates because to do so is the cultural norm of his world. It seems probable that the increasing prejudice in the UK is by the 'unprejudiced discriminator', who may be discouraged by the Race Relations Act of 1968, which unequivocally though mildly penalizes many forms of racialistic behaviour. A related difficulty is that it is rarely possible, without intensive investigation, to estimate the importance within an individual's value system and personality organization of his prejudiced attitudes.

Levinson (1964) differentiates *pseudo-democratic* and *openly anti-democratic* prejudice and, writing in 1950, argued that most prejudice in the USA in commerce, housing and social life generally was of the former and not the latter variety. More precisely, Levinson characterizes the openly anti-democratic prejudice by its component of hatred, violence and the active wish to subordinate a minority group. The pseudo-democratic prejudice is modified to appear to conform to democratic ideals – the hostility is denied, and the discriminatory practices are rationalized. For example, 'It's not that I'm prejudiced, but . . . .', or 'Jews have their rights, but . . .'. It is interesting that Sir Oswald Mosley in 1968 was constrained to deny that his political party was openly anti-democratic in the 1930s, and sought to persuade his critics that, for example, his party's anti-Semitism was neither racialist nor violent, but only in keeping with a policy of defending Britain from war with Germany. The rationalization was that 'Jewish interests were thrown in favour of war', and Jews must therefore be opposed.

Levison warns that the pseudo-democratic façade is little influenced by most propaganda and educational material which attacks prejudice and discrimination as 'race hatred', because there is *no* conscious animosity or hostility of which the individual is aware. The individual has effectively rationalized his beliefs and they appear to him to be in harmony with conventional democratic values. The problem of influencing him is less that of exposing the irrational basis of his rationalizations, than of minimizing his need for prejudice while increasing his active involvement with democratic values. A great part of the pseudo-democratic thinking, for example, the denial of opportunities to a minority group, segregation and exclusion, can in times of economic and social stress degenerate into openly anti-democratic attitudes and policies. In the UK in 1971 it seems probable that a shift in an anti-democratic direction from a pseudo-democratic position is taking place.

The issue presents the social psychologist with a delicate moral dilemma. What is the responsibility of a society to prevent the formation of anti-democratic or pseudo-democratic personalities? What is the duty of society to discourage those factors that discourage the change of attitudes in a socially harmonious direction? Technical competence suggests that it is possible to diminish these potentially disruptive and violent personality patterns. Social expedience suggests that we should.

The strategies adopted will also depend upon the extent to which the prejudice involved is considered to be a consequence of mental ill-health rather than the learning of a culture-pattern. Levinson (1964) found, for example, that of a sample of 121 psychiatric patients, the highly prejudiced had less ability to control their impulses, had shallower interpersonal relationships, and tended to depend less upon immediate personal experience than upon stereotypes and conventions in their attitudes to people. In times of stress they tended to weaken their grip upon reality and retreat into a fantasy world.

The authors of *The Authoritarian Personality* conclude:

'Countermeasures should take into account the whole structure of the prejudiced outlook . . . upon such phenomena as stereotypy, emotional coldness, identification with power, and general destructiveness. . . . Yet a moment's reflection will show that the therapeutic possibilities of individual psychology are severely limited.'

Doubtless there is a psychopathology of racialism, and many prejudiced people display symptoms of emotional and cognitive disturbance. But in a society like South Africa in which racialism is normal, it is not pathological to be a racialist. Indeed, it is pathological to be non-racialistic by the standards

L   161 of a racialist society. There is a gradation from situations in which racialism is predominantly socially sanctioned and culturally determined, to those in which society plays a small part and an individual's psychopathology is the major factor. But in all societies there is *some* racialism present even if it be little more than mildly chauvinistic suspicion towards an outgroup, which the more susceptible people utilize for the satisfaction of their unconscious needs and the lessening of their tensions.

One can therefore consider the feasibility of manipulating socio-cultural factors in order to anticipate and forestall potentially anti-democratic and prejudiced attitudes and behaviour. Although individual or group psychotherapy may be essential for a lasting and radical 'cure' for the racialism of a minority who are emotionally disturbed, this is impractical even for these at this time. Can society and culture be so ordered that the capacity of the ordinary citizen to understand himself – and therefore to understand and tolerate others – be increased? Can society harmlessly, or even usefully, deflect the hostile attitudes towards the victim-groups or altogether dissipate them? Even Freud, who often minimizes the power of culture to effect a radical diminution of man's propensity to destroy himself and his fellows, cautiously concedes that there has been 'a strengthening of intellect, which is beginning to govern instinctual life, and an internalization of the aggressive impulses, with all its consequent advantages and perils'. Who can foresee whether destructiveness and aggression, or civilization will succeed?

V. THE CHANGING OF SITUATIONAL DETERMINANTS

Underlying all attempts to change prejudice and discrimination by the manipulation of groups and group attitudes and values, is the fostering of contact between members of hostile or antipathetic groups. Contact is no guarantee of understanding; but lack of contact is a partial inducement to misunderstanding and fantasy. Even conflict can, in some circumstances, be useful and creative in initiating a change towards a more stable and satisfying society. Where conflict is natural and functional, for example, where one group is striving to improve its status and reduce its insecurity, this can (1) alter the social structure and make possible the beginnings of social change; (2) extend social communication between sections of a society that were insulated from each other, as a dialogue between American whites and non-whites is opening in the USA, although it is still shrill and ugly, and such a dialogue has yet to begin in South Africa; (3) enhance social solidarity among the lower-status groups, as is happening among American Negroes and among non-whites (to a less extent?) in South Africa; (4) facilitate personal identity, in that it offers a means for protest, assertion and the possibility of success, however limited (Himes, 1966).

It is the nature and quality of contact, not its frequency, that determines its effect upon the individual's attitudes and behaviour. It is paradoxical that there is probably more casual interracial contact in South Africa than in most multi-racial states, yet it would be a feat of irresponsibility to argue that tace attitudes and behaviour in South Africa are benign. Contact does not necessarily diminish prejudice, nor does it inevitably increase understanding and sympathy. Contact will *tend* to change attitudes when it generates – or increases – the expectation that change is probable; otherwise contact can be superficial, casual, tense or hostile and is more likely to increase than decrease prejudice.

Simpson and Yinger (1965) have summarized the main effects of contact:

'(i) Equal status contact . . . is likely to reduce prejudice;
(ii) Stereotype-breaking contacts that show minority groups in roles not usually associated with them reduce prejudice;
(iii) Contacts that bring people of minority and majority groups together in functionally important activities reduce prejudice.'

The development of equal-status contact as a means of reducing prejudice. A striking example of equal-status contact was experienced by many soliders of the USA towards the end of World War II when platoons of Negroes were attached in terms of complete equality to white companies. This policy followed an executive order of President Roosevelt, which declared:

'I do hereby reaffirm the policy of the US that there shall be no discrimination in the employment of workers in defence industries or government, because of race, creed, colour or national origin. . . .'

An army needed to be raised, industry was needed to supply it, and the state could not afford to lose the services of any person. The problems of race relations in the army were similar to those in the rest of American society, and the responses of both Negro and white soldiers reveal, in rarely-reported detail, the successes and failures of this 'experiment in race relations'. Officers and sergeants in twenty-four companies that had Negro platoons were interviewed on their attitudes towards racial separation in the army, and an overwhelming majority of the white soldiers, from the North or from the South, approved of Negro soldiers being segregated in separate units, the most frequent reason given being 'the fear of friction'. Yet, in answer to the question, 'Some army divisions have companies which include Negro platoons and white platoons. How would you feel about it if your outfit was set up like that?' the proportion of white enlisted men who would 'dislike it very much' was only 7% in a company with a Negro platoon, increasing to 62% in units with no coloured platoons in white companies. After some time a sample of platoon sergeants in 24 companies that had Negro platoons were asked, 'Has your feeling changed since having served in the same unit with coloured soldiers?' More than three-quarters replied 'Yes, have become more favourable'. None replied that their feelings had become less favourable or more unfavourable. In answer to the questions, 'How well did the coloured soldiers in this company perform in combat?' more than 80% replied, 'Very well', and only 1% gave the mildly unfavourable answer, 'Not so well'. A platoon sergeant from South Carolina expressed the changing attitudes:

'When I heard about it, I said I'd be damned if I'd wear the same shoulder patch they did. After that first day when we saw how they fought, I changed my mind. They're just like any of the other boys to us.'

The authors of the study *The American Soldier* (Stouffer *et al.*, 1965) observed that although the integration of whites and coloured soldiers was imperfect, it could not be expected that it would be because the army was not insulated from the conflicts and strains of civilian life. Nevertheless, even men who initially objected to integrated units accepted them and in many cases their attitudes improved. Indeed it seens no exaggeration to write of 'the revolution in attitudes that took place among these men as a result of enforced contacts'.

Of course, this study does not answer the question whether enforced contacts would ameliorate attitudes in other situations. The peculiarity of this situation was that the demands and dangers of total war made it impossible to permit choice to those with hostile attitudes and the only practical and expedient policy was to insist that all soldiers were treated as having equal status regardless of their race. The authors discuss the recommendations of an official board that investigated the major points of racial friction encountered in the army, and while neither denying nor minimizing the difficulties, tensions and misunderstandings that a policy of integration entails, agree with the board that a policy of integration is the only policy possible within the context of the American democratic tradition. Further, the alternative policy of allowing separation and discrimination to continue is more likely to encourage racialism and prejudice than to avoid friction points.

Few studies of behaviour change in situations of equal-status contact include a wide range of everyday activities, but housing is one area of life that permits 'real life' study. Deutsch and Collins (1951) investigated two housing schemes in the neighbouring cities of New York and Newark. The projects in Newark housed both Negro and white families in segregated units. In New York Negro and white families were assigned to apartment buildings without regard to their race. The housing schemes were for poor families, all were in mainly Negro neighbourhoods, 'considerably deteriorated and characterized by much delinquency', with similar proportions of white and Negro families.

Interviews with the housewives suggested that prejudice was sharply reduced in the integrated projects, and this finding was supported by an examination of the numbers of tenants who moved away and their reasons, the housewives' interracial experiences before they moved into the apartments, and a comparison of the housewives who knew about the pattern of occupancy before they applied for an apartment with those who did not know. The authors consider that their investigations

> 'discredit a notion that has characterized much of social-science thinking in the field of race relations . . . that "stateways cannot change folkways" . . . Official policy, executed without equivocation, can result in large changes in behaviour despite intitial resistance to that policy.'

The principal changes arose less from deliberate policy to create better race relations than from the emergence of many situations in which equal-status contact was inevitable and 'physical and functional proximity' inescapable. In the integrated projects more than 95% of the women interviewed indicated that they were likely to get to know coloured people, compared with 30% and 21% of the housewives in the segregated bi-racial schemes. This striking difference is accounted for by the places the housewives described as most likely meeting-places: the actual buildings in which they lived, outside on benches and the laundry in or near the buildings. In the segregated projects it was less easy for those informal meeting-places to become equally available to both races. Similar differences appeared in neighbourly activities such as helping with another woman's shopping, visiting, going to the movies together, sewing clubs. In the integrated projects many of the white women were neighbourly in this way, but in the segregated projects, very few. Interviews with the Negro housewives and their children confirmed these different patterns of contact: 'in effect, living in the integrated projects produces a *behavioural* change with respect to race relations for many of the white people'. The different housing schemes developed group norms or standards about racial issues. In the integrated projects white housewives *expected* approval and support if they were friendly with a Negro resident, and by contrast, in the segregated projects the housewife expected to be socially ostracized by the other white women if she happened to be friendly with a Negro. But the most striking evidence of the development of norms was the friendship patterns of the children. The children in segregated projects went to unsegregated elementary schools and had the opportunity to mix with members of the other race. Yet no such child, whatever his choice of friends in the school, would have a child of another race as a friend in activities within the project. On the other hand, children in the integrated projects played together in the project as freely as in school, and visited one another's homes.

Finally, the effects upon interracial attitudes in the projects differed. Through their experiences in the integrated projects, white housewives tended to shift their attitudes towards Negroes in a more favourable direction, and few of the tenants in the segregated projects did so. The housewives in the integrated projects were far less prejudiced than those in the segregated projects, and among the housewives in the integrated projects 'their experiences in the project with Negro people have become partially *generalized,* so that they now have more favourable attitudes towards Negroes as a group', even outside the project.

> Interviews illustrate the changing attitudes. One woman said: 'I thought I was moving into the heart of Africa. . . . I had always heard things about how they were. . . . they were dirty, drink a lot . . . were like savages. Living with them my ideas have changed altogether. They're just people . . . they're not any different.'

The authors claim their findings are consistent with the growing evidence that equal-status contacts can change prejudiced attitudes and discriminatory behaviour, provided that (1) the behaviour of the 'objects of prejudice' does not conform with the beliefs of the prejudiced; (2) the amount and closeness of the contact is sufficiently realistic and compelling to resist the tendency to become distorted to fit the old stereotypes; (3) the contact is in such conditions that the prejudiced person cannot interpret the behaviour of the object of prejudice as due to the situation rather than to his personal qualities. If the friendly Negro store-clerk is primarily behaving as a store-clerk *should* behave, then his friendliness is unlikely to have any effect upon the attitudes of a prejudiced person; (4) the prejudiced person is exposed to social influences which strongly and clearly conflict with his retaining his prejudiced behaviour.

The educational system is perhaps the most promising area

in which to ensure equal-status contact, though the effects upon the attitudes of the pupils or students will depend upon many factors, for instance, the attitudes of school and education officials, the prevailing social atmosphere, the attitudes of parents and others in the neighbourhood, the age at which the contact began, the numbers of children of different races. . . . Desegregation in the USA at school, college and university level encourages mild optimism. Coles (1963), for example, found that there were marked changes in attitudes even by the most segregation-supporting adolescents, and the pressures of everyday experience and constant meeting can initiate a cumulative process of improving racial attitudes. But a decrease in prejudice is not inevitable. If for example there are too few members of a minority group, they can be easily isolated, regarded as exceptions, and the stereotypes about them remain unchanged. On the other hand, when there are too many, status conflicts between the majority and the minority can develop. The educational system is a part of the total society and is influenced by the total society's traditions, weaknesses, tensions, power structure and pattern of change. It is naïve to assume that education can by itself 'cure' racialism, but it can provide opportunities to practise non-racialism in a practical and neutral context, and to strengthen the non-racialist.

The approaches above described are not alternatives, neither are they a complete solution to the problems of race relations. The psychological and sociological approaches are complementary. Moreover, their success or failure depend upon the vigour, skill and flexibility of the minority and majority groups in initiating and maintaining the impetus for broad changes in the economic and social system *as a whole* – both in its structure and its value-system. Indeed, the importance of the Negro revolution, and of the efforts of other minority groups in discriminatory societies, is in providing the leverage for change over a social front wider than that narrowly included in 'race relations'.[1]

Fanon's *The Wretched of the Earth* proposes a psychiatric justi-

[1] Clark (1963), in an address entitled 'The role of the social sciences in desegregation', indicated some of the critical factors associated with effective and ineffective desegregation in the USA. One of the more important was the firm and unequivocal intention of authority to enforce desegregation.

fication for violence. Only by dramatically, violently bursting out of their immobility and rejecting feelings of defeat can dominated groups assert themselves, show that they are human beings with their own autonomy, and begin to create a meaningful sense of identity. Fanon writes that 'voilence is a cleansing force. It frees the native from his inferiority complex and from his despair and inaction; it makes him fearless and restores his self-respect'. He appears to be arguing that violence is not solely a political weapon, but is a psychological weapon of even greater potency.

Few racial situations have been without their violence: few dominated peoples have freed themselves without violence. It may be accepted that some measure of violence can act as a catalyst to accelerate economic and social change. But the results of violence are frequently unpredictable and unforeseen, so as a political weapon its employment is may be as hazardous to the wielders as to the victims. Wolfgang (1970) observes that 'violence is a means of seeking power and may be defined as an act of despair committed when the door is closed to alternative resolutions. It comes from the failure to have a more abundant repertoire of means to gain a goal' – it is here described as social technique. The psychologist should add, however, that when men and women act out of a sense of despair (which may be realistic or fantasy), their behaviour may be less precisely appropriate to reaching their goal and ideals than if they had acted without a sense of despair. Moreover, much contemporary violence seems to be derived less from a sense of despair, or even a search for identity, than from the deep frustration of living insecure and stunted lives. Revenge – be it the crudity of a riot and looting, or the expropriation of the goods and chattels of defenceless groups – has little political value, and its psychological aftermath is frequently guilt, depression and shame.

The psychologist cannot *as psychologist* enter the debate of violent versus non-violent methods of social change. He is no more (or less) free to make political judgements than any other citizen. But, *as a psychologist* he must warn both those who resort to violence to remedy their wrongs, and those who maintain a system that provokes such violence, that violence once aroused is rarely contained.

Freud warned in his *Civilization and its Discontents* of the dangers of violence:

'Civilized society is perpetually menaced with disintegration through this primary hostility of men towards one another. . . . Culture has to call up every possible reinforcement in order to erect barriers against the aggressive instincts of men and hold their manifestations in check by reaction-formations in men's minds.'

V. INTEGRATION OR AUTONOMY — A POLITICAL AND SOCIAL DILEMMA

Is it arguable, however, that ultimately the extremists such as the Black Muslims or the devotees of *apartheid* might be partially correct? It has been suggested that integration versus segregation is a false issue, and a liberal, Handlin (1966), closely approaches the positions of Verwoerd and Malcolm X when he advocates the unpopular argument that apartness is not necessarily an attempt to assert the superiority of one group and the inferiority of another. Handlin argues that apartness can be an innocent recognition of different cultural back grounds and ways of life, which integration denies, demanding from both minority and majority groups an impossible surrender of identity.

This seductively attractive argument, beguiling both to racialists and to the tolerant, conceals a fatal drop of poison like the apple rashly tasted by the Sleeping Beauty. At its worst, separation or segregation is a euphemism for a policy of maintaining equality and the exploitation of politically and socially weaker groups. At its most plausible, the case for segregation is that it is the only way to avoid friction between peoples with differing cultural standards and ways of life. Worsthorne, in a provocative article entitled 'Integration can't work, so let's start thinking', deplores racialism but argues despairingly that:

'what is needed urgently is that some of the intelligence, imagination, energy and compassion which men of good-will have hitherto wasted in seeking to demonstrate how the races can live together should be concentrated instead on studying how they can be helped to live apart. . . .'

On the contrary, in a world that is increasingly composed of interdependent units, there is *no* alternative to the races living together. *Apartheid* on a large scale is not compatible as a long-term policy with either civic order or mental health. There can be no escape from contact with alien people and alien ideas, and *apartheid*'s ideological basis fails to appreciate that the psychological origins of suspicion, hostility and race hatred are rooted in the very process of segregation.

From the standpoint of the minority groups, integration may also seem a false issue, but for reasons that differ from those given by Handlin. Malcolm X *suspected* much integration for its superficial solution to a deep problem: 'A desegregated cup of coffee, a theatre, public toilets – the whole range of hypocritical "integration" – these are not atonement.' But even in the context of scientific discussion, Malcolm X's suspicions are relevant to policy. The damage that has been done by discriminatory social systems is too severe to be remedied by the token abolition of minor irritations. Race prejudice and discrimination, in their organized and institutionalized forms, have destroyed societies and stunted personalities. Peoples have been estranged and alienated, compelled to maintain themselves as outcast communities of Jews, Negroes . . . they have been constrained to despise their own identities, and to feel shame for qualities of which they should – like all human beings – have felt proud.

A psychologist can reasonably demand that in the interest of social and individual health and stability – no less than in the interests of justice – no person nor group should be an outcast; nor should any person or group be made to forego his sense of identity. Moreover,

'for those who wish to assimilate, there should be no artificial barriers placed in their way; for those who wish to maintain ethnic integrity, their efforts should be met with tolerance and appreciation.' (Allport, 1954.)

No psychologist seeks to blur the differences between peoples. On the contrary: he believes that there is every justification for mankind to be proud of, and to take pleasure from, the rich repertory of diverse backgrounds, talents and temperaments. What Sartre, in his *Portrait of an Anti-Semite*, asserts of anti-

171

Semitism applies with equal force to other forms of intolerance:

> 'Anti-Semitism . . . could not exist in a classless society. It demonstrates the *separation* of men, and their isolation in the midst of the community, the conflict of interests and the splitting up of passions.'

Mankind has to learn to accept that '. . . *the man* does not exist: there are Jews, Protestants and Catholics, Frenchmen, Englishmen and Germans, Whites, Blacks and Yellows . . . .' Race prejudice will lose its virulence when the diversity of mankind is appreciated and enjoyed, and it becomes understood that the interests of mankind are inextricably related to the welfare of each and every individual.

References

ADAM, W. A.   The Negro patient in psychiatric treatment. *Amer. J. Ortho-Psychiatry*, 1950, **20,** 305–10.

ADINARAYANIAH, S. P.   *The Psychology of Colour Prejudice.* Unpublished M.A. thesis, University of London, 1939.

ADINARAYANIAH, S. P.   'A research in colour prejudice', *B. J. Psych.*, 1941, 31, 217–9.

ADORNO, T. W. *et al.*   *The Authoritarian Personality*, New York, John Wiley, 1964.

ALBINO, R. S. AND THOMPSON, V. J.   'The effects of sudden weaning on Zulu children', *B. J. Med. Psych.*, 1956, XXIX, 177–210.

ALLPORT, G. W.   *The Nature of Prejudice*, Cambridge, Mass., Addison-Wesley, 1958.

ALLPORT, G. W.   'Prejudice in modern perspective', in *Personality or Social Encounter*, Boston, Beacon Press, 1960.

ANON.   *South Africa and the Rule of Law*, Geneva, International Commission of Jurists, 1960.

ARENDT, H.   *The Origins of Totalitarianism*, New York, Meridian Books, 1958.

ATHEY, K. R. *et al.*   'Two experiments showing the effect of the interviewer's racial background on responses to questionnaires concerning racial issues', *J. App. Psychol.*, 1960, 244–6.

AUERBACH, F. E.   *The Power of Prejudice in South African Education*, Cape Town, A. A. Balkema, 1966.

AUSUBEL, D. P.   *Maori Youth: A Psychoethnological Study of Cultural Deprivation*, New York, Holt, Rinehart & Winston, 1965.

BALDWIN, J.   *The Fire Next Time*, London, Michael Joseph, 1963.

BANTON, M.   'Race as a social category', *Race*, 1966, **8,** 1, 1–16. *Race Relations*, London, Social Science Paperbacks, 1967.

BARATZ, S. S.   'Effect of Race experiments, instructions, and comparison population upon the level of reported anxiety in Negro subjects', *J. Personality & Soc. Psychol.*, 1967, **7,** 194–6.

BERNSTEIN, B. B. 'Some sociological determinants of perception: an enquiry into subcultural differences', *B. J. Sociol.*, 1958, **9,** 159–74.
'Linguistic codes, hesitation phenomena and intelligence', *Language and Speech*, 1962, **5,** 31–00.
'Social class, linguistic codes and grammatical elements', *Language and Speech*, 1962a, **5,** 221–00.

BETTELHEIM, B. 'Individual and mass behaviour in extreme situations', *J. Abn. Soc. Psychol.*. 1943, **38,** 417–52.

BETTELHEIM, B. AND JANOWITZ *Social change and prejudice*, New York, Collier-Macmillan, 1964.

BIESHEUVEL, S. *Race, culture and personality*, Johannesburg, S.A.I.R.R. 1959.

BLOOM, L. 'Self-concepts and social status in South Africa', *J. Soc. Psychol.*, 1960, **51,** 103–12.

BLOOM, L. *et al.* 'An interdisciplinary study of social, moral and political attitudes of white and non-white South African university students', *J. Soc. Psychol.*, 1961, **54,** 3–12.
'Education for Africans in South Africa', *Integrated Education*, 1965, III, 4/5, 89–94.

BOAS, F. *The Mind of Primitive Man*, Glencoe, Illinois, The Free Press, 1965.
Race, Language and Culture, Glencoe, Illinois, The Free Press, 1966.

BRODY, E. B. 'Colour and identity conflict in young boys: observations of Negro mothers and sons in urban Baltimore', *Psychiatry*, 1963, **26,** 2, 188–201.

BROOKES, E. H. AND MACAULEY, J. B. *Civil Liberties in South Africa*, Cape Town, Oxford U.P., 1958.

BRYANT, E. C. *et al.* 'Responses on racial attitudes as affected by interviewers of different ethnic groups', *J. Soc. Psychol.*, 1966, **70(1),** 95–100.

BURT, C. 'The mental differences between children', in Cox, C. B. and Dyson, A. E. (eds.), *Black Paper Two*, London, The Critical Quarterly Society, 1970.

CALNEK, M. 'Racial factors in the countertransference: the Black therapist and the Black client', *Amer. J. Orthopsychiatry*, Jan. 1970, **40,** 1, 39–46.

CAMPBELL, E. Q. Moral discomfort and racial segregation: An examination of the Myrdal hypothesis, *Social Forces*, 1961, **39,** 228–34.

CLARK, K. B. Clash of cultures in the classroom. In Weinberg, M.

(ed.), *Learning Together – A Book on Integrated Education*, Chicago, Integrated Education Associates, 1964.

CLARK, K. B. AND M. P. 'Segregation as a factor in the racial identification of Negro pre-school children: A preliminary report', *J. Exp. Educ.*, 1939, **9**, 161–3.
'The development of consciousness of self and the emergence of racial identification in Negro pre-school children', *J. Soc. Psychol.*, 1939, **10**, 591–9.

COHN, N. 'The myth of the demonic conspiracy of Jews in mediaeval and modern Europe', in de Rueck, A. and Knight, J. (eds.), *Caste and Race: Comparative Approaches*, London, Churchill, 1967.

COLES, R. *The Desegregation of Southern Schools: A psychiatric study*, New York, Anti-defamation League, 1963.

COHN, N. *Warrant for Genocide*, Harmondsworth, Penguin, 1970.

COLES, R. 'Northern children under desegregation', *Psychiatry*, 1968, **31**, 1, 1–16.
Children of Crisis – a Study of Courage and Fear, London, Faber & Faber, 1968a.

COMER, J. P. 'Research and the Black Backlash', *Amer. J. Orthopsychiatry*, Jan. 1970, **40**, 1, 8–11.

COON, C. S. *The Living Races of Man*, London, Cape, 1966.

COOPER, E. AND JAHODA, M. 'The evasion of propaganda: How prejudiced people respond to anti-prejudice propaganda', *J. Psychol.*, 1947, **23**, 15–25.

COX, O. C. *Caste, Class and Race*, New York, Monthly Review Press, 1959.

CRIJNS, A. G. J. *Race relations and race attitudes in South Africa*, Nijmegen, Janssen, 1959.

DANIEL, W. W. *Racial discrimination in England*, Harmondsworth, Penguin, 1968.

DANZIGER, K. 'Self interpretation of group differences in values (Natal, South Africa)', *J. Soc. Psychol.*, 1958, **47**, 317–25.
'Validation of a measure of self-rationalisation', *J. Soc. Psychol.*, 1963, **59**, 17–28.

DAVIS, A. AND DOLLARD, J. *Children of Bondage*, New York, Harper Torchbooks, 1964.

DAVIS, M. 'Results of personality tests given to Negroes in Northern and Southern US and in Halifax, Canada, *Phylon*, 1964, **25**, 4, 362–9.

DEAKIN, N. L. *et al.* 'Colour and the 1966 General Election', *Race*, 1966, VIII, 1, 17–43.
Colour, Citizenship and British Society, London, Panther Books, 1970.

DEDIJER, V.　*The Road to Sarajevo*, London, MacGibbon & Kee, 1967.

DERBYSHIRE, R. L.　'United States Negro identity conflict', *Sociol. & Social Res.*, 1966, **51,** 1, 63–77.

DERBYSHIRE, R. L. AND BRODY, E. B.　'Marginality, identity and behaviour in the American Negro: A fundamental analysis', *Int. J. Soc. Psychiatry*, 1964, **10,** 1, 7–13.

DEUTSCH, M.　*Psychologists comment on current IQ controversy: heredity versus environment.* Statement by Society for the Psychological Study of Social Issues. May 1969, Ann Arbor, Mich.

DEUTSCH, M. AND COLLINS, M. E.　*Inter-racial housing: A psychological evaluation of a social experiment.* St Paul's, University of Minnesota Press, 1951.

DE VOS, G.　'The psychology of purity and pollution as related to social self-identity and caste', in: de Rueck, A. and Knight, J. (eds.), *Caste and Race: Comparative Approaches*, London, Churchill, 1967.

DOLLARD, J.　*Caste and class in a Southern Town*, New York, Doubleday Anchor, 1957.

DOXEY, G. V.　*The Industrial Colour Bar in South Africa*, Cape Town, Oxford U.P., 1961.

DREGER, R. M. AND MILLER, K. S.　'Comparative psychological studies of Negroes and whites in the US', *Psych. Bull.*, 1960, **57,** 361–402.
'Comparative psychological studies of Negroes and whites in the US: 1959–1965', *Psychol. Bull. Monograph Supp.*, 1968, **70,** No. 3, Part 2, 1–58.

ELKINS, S. M.　*Slavery: A problem in American institutional and intellectual life*, New York, Grosset & Dunlap, 1963.

ENSOR, R.　*England: 1870–1917.* London, Oxford U.P., 1949.

ERIKSON, E. H.　*Identity: Youth and Crisis*, New York, Norton, 1968.

EYSENCK, H. J.　'Primary social attitudes. A comparison of attitude patterns in England, Germany and Sweden', *J. Abn. Soc. Psychol.*, 1953, **48,** 563–8.
The Psychology of Politics, London, Routledge, 1954.

FANON, F.　*The Wretched of the Earth*, London, MacGibbon & Kee, 1965.
Black Skin, White Masks. London, Paladin Books, 1970.

FITZPATRICK, J. P.　*The Transvaal from Within*, London, Heinemann, 1900.

FLUGEL, J. C.   *Man, Morals and Society*, London, Peregrine, 1965.

FOOT, P.   *Immigration and Race in British Politics*, Harmondsworth, Penguin, 1965.

FRENKEL-BRUNSWIK, E.   'A study of prejudice in children', *Human Relations*, 1949, **1**, 295–306.

GAIER, E. T. AND WAMBACH, J. S.   'Self-evaluation of personality assets and liabilities of Southern white and Negro students', *J. Soc. Psychol.*, 1960, **51**, 135–43.

GENOVESE, E. D.   *The Political Economy of Slavery: Studies in the Economy and Society of the Slave South*. London, MacGibbon & Kee, 1966.

GLOVER, E.   *War, Sadism and Pacifism*, London, Allen & Unwin, 1947.

GOODMAN, M. E.   *Race Awareness in Young Children*, New York, Collier-Macmillan, 1964.

GORDON, E. B.   'Mentally ill West Indian immigrants', *B. J. Psychiatry*, 1965, III (478), 877–87.

GOSSETT, T. F.   *Race: The History of an Idea in America*, New York, Schocken Books, 1965.

GRAY, R.   *The Two Nations: Aspects of the Development of Race Relations in the Rhodesias and Nyasaland*, London, Oxford U.P., 1960.

GRAY, S. W. AND KLAUS, R. A.   'An experimental pre-school program for culturally deprived children', *Child Development*, 1965, **36**, 869–86.

GREGOR, A. J.   'Race relations, frustrations and aggression', *Revue Internationale de Sociologie*, 1965, Série 2, II, 2, 90–112.

GRIER, W. AND COBBS, P.   *Black Rage*, New York, Basic Books, 1968.

HALDANE, J. B. S.   Comment, in Comas, J., ' "Scientific Racism" again?', *Current Anthropology*, 1961, **2**, 4, 303–14; 313–40 (comments).

HANDLIN, O.   'The goals of integration', *Daedalus*, 1966, **95**, 1, 268–84.

HANSEN, C. F.   *Addendum: A five year report on desegregation in the Washington DC schools*. New York, Anti-Defamation League, 1960.
'Scholastic performance of Negro and white pupils in the integrated public schools of the District of Columbia', *J. Educ. Sociol.*, 1963, **36**, 287–91.

HASHMI, F.   'Mores, migration and mental illness', in Wolstenholme, G. E. W. and O'Connor, M. (eds.), *Immigration: Medical and Social Aspects*, London, Churchill, 1966.

HAVIGHURST, R. J. 'Minority subcultures and the law of effect', *American Psychologist*, 1970, **25,** 4, 313-22.

HILL, C. J. *How Colour Prejudiced is Britain?* London, Gollancz, 1965.

HIMES, J. S. 'The functions of racial conflict', *Social Forces*, 1966, **45,** 1, 1-10.

HOLLEMAN, J. F. *et al.* 'A Rhodesian white minority under threat', *J. Soc. Psychol.*, 1962, **57,** 315-38.

HOOPER, R. (ed.) *Colour in Britain*, London, BBC, 1965.

HOROWITZ, E. L. 'The development of attitudes towards the Negro', *Archives of Psychology*, 1936, No. 194.

HOROWITZ, I. L. *Three Worlds of Development*, New York, Oxford U.P., 1966.

HOROWITZ, R. E. 'Racial aspects of self-identification in nursery school children', *J. Psychol.*, 1939, **7,** 91-9.

HORRELL, M. (ed.) *A Survey of race relations in South Africa*, Annual, Johannesburg, S.A.I.R.R.
Legislation and race relations, Johannesburg, 1963, S.A.I.R.R.
A decade of Bantu Education, Johannesburg, 1964, S.A.I.R.R.

HORWOOD, O. P. F. *The Social Framework of Economic Development in a Dual Society: The Case of South Africa*, Durban, Institute of Social Research, Univ. of Natal, 1962.

HUDSON, E. *et al.* *Anatomy of South Africa*, Johannesburg, Purnell, 1966.

HURWITZ, N. *The Economics of Bantu Education in South Africa*, Johannesburg, S.A.I.R.R., 1964.

HUTCHINS, R. M. *The Nature of Human Life*, Bulletin Center for the Study of Democratic Institutions of the Fund for the Republic, March 1961, No. 10.

HUTT, W. H. *The Economics of the Colour Bar*, London, André Deutsch, 1964.

'IMPERIALIST' *Cecil Rhodes, with Personal Reminiscences by Dr Jameson*, London, Chapman & Hall, 1897.

ISHERWOOD, J. B. *Racial contours*, Isle of Man, Times Press, 1966.

ISRAEL, W. H. *Colour and Community – a Study of Coloured Immigrants and Race Relations in an Industrial town*, Slough, Slough Council of Social Service, 1966.

JAHODA, G. 'Development of Scottish children's ideas and attitudes about other countries', *J. Soc. Psychol.*, 1962, **58,** 91-108.

JAHODA, M. *Race Relations and Mental Health*, Paris, UNESCO, 1960.

JAMES, W. *Principles of Psychology*, New York, Dover, 1950.

JANIS, I. L. *et al.* *Personality and Persuadability*, New Haven, Conn., Yale U.P., 1959.

JENSEN, A. R. 'How can we boost I.Q. and scholastic achievement?' *Harvard Educational Review*, (winter), 1969, **39**, 1–124.

JOHN, V. P. AND GOLDSTEIN, L. S. 'The social context of language acquisition', *Merrill-Palmer Quarterly*, 1964, **10**, 265–75.

JONES, E. *Othello's Countrymen: The African in English Renaissance Drama*, London, Oxford U.P., 1965.

KARDINER, A. AND OVESEY, L. *The Mark of Oppression: Explorations in the Personality of the American Negro*, New York, Meridian, 1965.

KARON, B. P. *The Negro Personality*, New York, Springer, 1958.

KIEV, A. 'Psychotherapeutic aspects of Pentecostal sects among West Indian immigrants to England', *B. J. Sociol.*, 1964, XV, 2, 129–39.

KLINEBERG, O. *Race and Psychology*, Paris, UNESCO, 1951.

KNUPFER, G. 'Portrait of the Underdog', *Public Opinion Quarterly*, 1947, **11**, 103–14.

KORTEN, F. F. *et al.* (eds.) *Psychology and the Problems of Society*, Washington, DC, American Psychological Association, 1970.

KOVEL, J. *White racism: A psychohistory*, London, Allen Lane–Penguin Press, 1970.

KUBIE, L. S. 'The ontogeny of racial prejudice', *J. of Nervous and Mental Diseases*, 1965, **141**, 3, 265–73.

KUPER, L. *Passive Resistance in South Africa*, New Haven, Yale U.P., 1960.
An African Bourgeoisie, New Haven, Yale U.P., 1965.

KUSHNICK, L. 'The implementation of anti-discrimination legislation: problems and proposals', in Second Annual Race Relations Conference: *The Absorption of Minorities: Research and its Translation into Action*, London, Institute of Race Relations, 1967.

KVARACEUS, W. C. *et al.* *Negro Self-concept: Implications for School and citizenship*, New York, McGraw Hill, 1965.

LANDES, R. 'A preliminary statement of a survey of Negro-white relationships in Britain', *Man.* Sept. 1952, p. 133.
'Race and recognition', *The Listener*, 1952a, Nov. 6, pp. 751, 763.

LANTERNARI, V. *The Religions of the Oppressed: A Study of Modern Messianic Cults*, New York, Alfred A. Knopf, 1963.

LAPIERE, R. T. 'Race Prejudice: France and Britain', *Social Forces*, 1928, **7**, 102–11.

LASKER, B. *Race Attitudes in Children*, New York, Holt, 1929.

LASSWELL, H. D. 'The policy orientations', in Lerner, D. *et al.* (eds.), *The Policy Sciences*, Stanford, Stanford U.P., 1965.

LEE, E. S. 'Negro intelligence and selective migration. A Philadelphia test of the Klineberg hypothesis', *Amer. Sociol. Rev.*, 1951, **16**, 227–33.

LEFCOURT, H. M. AND LADWIG, G. W. 'Alienation in Negro and white reformatory inmates', *J. Soc. Psychol.*, 1966, **68**, 152–9.

LESSER, G. H. *et al.* 'Mental abilities of children from different social-class and cultural groups', *Monographs of Soc. Res. Child Development*, 1965, **30**, 4, Series No. 102.

LEVER, H. 'An experimental modification of social distance in South Africa', *Human Relations*, May 1965, **18**, 2, 149–54.
Ethnic Attitudes of Johannesburg Youth, Johannesburg, University of Witwatersrand Press, 1968.

LEVINSON, D. J. 'The study of anti-Semitic ideology', in Adorno, T. W. *et al.*, op. cit., 1964.
'Psychological ill health in relation to potential Fascism: A study of psychiatric clinic patients', in Adorno, T. W. *et al.*, op. cit., 1964.

LEVI-STRAUSS, C. *Structural Anthropology*, New York, Basic Books, 1963.

LEWIS, O. *The Children of Sanchez*, Harmondsworth, Penguin, 1964.

LIFTON, R. J. *Thought Reform and the Psychology of Totalism*, New York, W. W. Norton, 1961.

LITTLE, K. L. *Negroes in Britain: a study of racial relations in English society*, London, Routledge and Kegan Paul, 1947.

LONG, H. H. 'The relative learning capacities of Negroes and whites', *J. Negro Education*, 1957, 26, 126–30.

MACRONE, I. D. 'The frontier traditions and race attitudes in South Africa', *Race Relations Journal* (Johannesburg), 1961, **28**, 19–30.
Race attitudes in South Africa: Historical, experimental and psychological studies, Johannesburg, Witwatersrand U.P., 1965 (1st ed. 1937).

MALCOLM X *The Autobiography of Malcolm X*, London, Hutchinson, 1966.

MALHERBE, E. G. *Educational Requirements for Economic Expansion.* Johannesburg, S.A.I.R.R., 1965.

MANDLE, W. F. *Anti-Semitism and the BUF*, London, Longmans, 1968.

MANNONI, O. *Prospero and Caliban: The Psychology of Colonisation*, New York, Praeger, 1964.

MAUCORPS, P. H. *et al.* *Les Français et le Racism*, Paris, Payot, 1965.

MAUSNER, B. AND J. 'A study of the anti-scientific attitude', *Scientific American*, Feb. 1955.

MAXWELL, N. G. A. *The Power of Negro Action*. London, privately published, no date.

MERTON, R. K. 'Discrimination and the American Creed', in MacIver, R. M. (ed.), *Discrimination and National Welfare*, New York, Institute of Religious and Social Studies, 1949.

MILLER, J. O. 'Disadvantaged families: despair to hope', in KORTEN, F. F., *et al.* (eds.), op. cit.

MILLS, C. W. *The Sociological Imagination*, New York, Oxford U.P., 1959.

MOSHER, D. L. AND SCODEL, A. 'Relations between ethno-centricism in children and authoritarian rearing practices of their mothers', *Child Development*, 1960, **31**, 369–76.

MULVANEY, D. J. 'The prehistory of the Australian Aborigine', *Scientific American*, March 1966, **214**, 3, 84–93.

MUSSEN, P. H. 'Some personality and social factors related to changes in children's attitudes towards Negroes', *J. Abn. Soc. Psychol.*, 1950, **45**, 423–41.

MUSSEN, P. H. AND NAYLOR, H. K. 'The relationships between overt and fantasy aggression', *J. Abn. Soc. Psychol.*, 1954, **49**, 235–40.

MYRDAL, G. *An American Dilemma*, New York, McGraw-Hill, 1964.

NASH, M. 'Race and the ideology of race', *Current Anthropology*, 1962, **3**, 286–8.

N'DAW, A. Peut-on parler d'une pensée Africaine? *Présence Africaine*.

NKRUMAH, K. *Africa Must Unite*, London, Heinemann, 1963.

PASSOW, A. H. (ed.) *Education in Depressed Areas*, New York, Columbia U.P., 1963.

PASSOW, A. H. *et al.* (eds.) *Education of the Disadvantaged*, New York, Holt, Rinehart and Winston, 1967.

PETTIGREW, T. F. 'Personality and socio-cultural factors in intergroup attitudes, a cross-national comparison', *J. Conflict. Resolution*, 1958, **2**, 29–42.

A Profile of the Negro American, Princeton, New Jersey, D. van Nostrand, 1964.

PIAGET, J. *Judgement and Reasoning in the Child*, Patterson, New Jersey, Littlefield, Adams, 1959.

RADIN, P. *Primitive man as Philosopher*, New York, Dover, 1957.

REX, J. *Race Relations in Sociological Theory*, London, Weidenfeld & Nicolson, 1970.

REX, J. AND MOORE, R. *Race, Community and Conflict: A Study of Sparkbrook*, London, Oxford U.P., 1966.

RICHMOND, A. H. *The Colour Problem – A Study of Racial Relations*, Harmondsworth, Penguin, 1961.

RIESSMAN, F. *The Culturally Deprived Child*, New York, Harper & Row, 1962.

(ed.) *Learning Together*, Chicago, Integrated Education Associates, 1964.

ROACH, J. L. AND GURSSLIN, O. R. 'An evaluation of the concept "culture of poverty" ', *Social Forces*, 1967, **45**, 3, 383–92.

ROBB, J. H. *The Working-class Anti-Semite*, London, Tavistock, 1954.

ROBERTSON, H. M. '150 years of economic contact between white and black', *South African Journal of Economics*, 1934, II, 4, 403–25; 1935, III, 1, 3–25.

ROGERS, C. A. AND FRANZ, C. *Racial Themes in Rhodesia: The Attitudes and Behaviour of the White Population*, New Haven, Yale U.P., 1962.

ROHRER, J. H. AND EDMONDSON, M. S. *The Eighth Generation Grows Up*, New York, Harper Torchbooks, 1964.

ROKEACH, M. AND MEZEI, L. 'Race and shared belief as factors in social choice', *Science*, 1966, 151, 167–72.

ROSE, E. J. B. *et al.* *Colour and Citizenship*, London, Oxford U.P., 1969.

ROSEN, B. C. 'Race, ethnicity and the achievement syndrome', *Amer. Sociol. Rev.*, 1959, **24**, 47–60.

RUBIN, I. 'The reduction of prejudice through laboratory training', *J. of Applied Behavioral Science*, 1967, **3**, 1, 29–50.

SETTLER, J. M. 'Statistical re-analysis of Canady's "The effect of 'rapport' on the IQ: A new approach to the problem of racial IQ" ', *Psychol. Reports*, 1966, **19**, 3, 1203–6.

SEGAL, R. *The Race War*, Harmondsworth, Penguin Books, 1967.

SELECT COMMITTEE ON RACE RELATIONS AND IMMIGRATION. *The Problems of Coloured School-leavers*, 4 vols, H.M.S.O., 1969.

SHIBUTANI, T. 'Reference groups as perspectives', *Amer. J. Sociol.* 1955, **60,** 562–9.

SHIBUTANI, T. AND KWAN, K. M. *Ethnic Stratification – A Comparative, Approach,* New York, Macmillan, 1965.

SHUEY, A. *The Testing of Negro Intelligence,* Lynchburg Va, Bell, 1966.

SIMPSON, G. E. AND YINGER, J. M. *Racial and Cultural Minorities: An Analysis of Prejudice and Discrimination,* New York, Harper & Row, 1965.

SIVANANDAN, A. AND SCRUTON, M. *Register of Research on Commonwealth Immigrants in Britain,* London, Institute of Race Relations, 1967.

SMART, M. 'Confirming Klineberg's suspicion', *Amer. Psychologist,* 1963, **18,** 621.

STEVENSON, H. W. AND STEWART, E. C. 'A developmental study of racial awareness in young children', *Child Development,* 1958, **29,** 399–409.

STOUFFER, S. A. *Communism, Conformity and Civil Liberties,* New York, Doubleday, 1955.

STOUFFER, S. A. *et al. The American Soldier: Vol. I: Adjustment during Army Life,* New York, John Wiley Science Editions, 1965.

SUNDKLER, B. G. M. *Bantu Prophets in South Africa,* London, Oxford U.P., 1961.

SUTTIE, I. D. *The Origins of Love and Hate,* Harmondsworth, Penguin, 1960.

TANSER, H. A. *The Settlement of Negroes in Kent County, Ontario, and a Study of the Mental Capacity of their Descendants,* Chatham, Ontario, Shephard, 1949.

TEMPELS, P. *Bantu Philosophy,* Paris, Présence Africaine, 1959.

THOMAS, L.-V. *Les Idéologies Négro-Africaines d'Aujourd'hui,* Dakar, L'Université de Dakar, 1965.

UNESCO 'Proposals on the biological aspects of race', *Int. Soc. Sci. J.,* 1965, XVIII, 1, 157–161.
Apartheid: Its Effect on Education, Science, Culture and Information, Paris, UNESCO, 1967.

VAN DEN BERGHE, P. L. 'The dynamics of racial prejudice: An ideal-type dichotomy', *Social Forces,* 1958, **37,** 138–41.
'Miscegenation in South Africa', *Cahiers d'Etudes Africaines,* 1960, **4,** 68–84.
South Africa: A Study in Conflict, Middletown, Conn., Wesleyan U.P., 1965.

VONTRESS, C. E. 'The Negro personality reconsidered', *J. Negro Educ.*, 1966, **36,** 3, 210–17.

WESTERMANN, D. *The African Today and Tomorrow*, London, Oxford U.P., 1949.

WHITE, R. K. ' "Black Boy" – A value analysis', *J. Abn. Soc. Psychol.*, 1947, **42,** 440–61.

WILLIAMS, J. A. AND WIENIR, P. L. 'A re-examination of Myrdal's rank-order of discrimination', *Soc. Problems*, 1947, **14,** 4, 443–54.

WODDIS, J. *Africa: The Roots of Revolt*, London, Lawrence & Wishart, 1960.

WOLFGANG, M. E. 'Violence and human behavior', in Korten, F. F., op. cit., 1970.

WRIGHT, N. 'The economics of race', *Amer. J. Econ. Sociol.*, 1967, **26,** 1–12.

Further Reading

An attempt has been made here to indicate some of the main sources – factual or controversial.

1. Race-Reality and Myth

BUETTNER–JANUSCH, J., *Origins of Man: Physical Anthropology*, Wiley, 1966. An unusually clear and complete account of man's evolution, well illustrating the biological significance and nature of race.

MEAD, M. *et al.* (eds.), *Science and the Concept of Race*, Columbia University Press, 1968.

MONTAGU, A. (ed.), *The Concept of Race*, Collier-Macmillan, 1964. *Man's Most Dangerous Myth: The Fallacy of Race*, Meridian Books, 1965. Mead's and Montagu's books provide a thorough and modern account of the value and the limitations of the concept of race, and integrate biological and anthropological points of view.

2. Racism – its origins and validity

COMAS, J., 'Scientific Racism again?', *Current Anthropology*, 1961, **2**, 4, 303–14, 314–40. A vigorous debate between supporters and opponents of the view that 'race' is a useful concept to explain human behaviour.

COX, O. C., *Caste, Class and Race*, Monthly Review Press. A major analysis of the origins and development of modern racialism. Well documented and argued with persuasive clarity.

MEMMI, A., 'Essai de Définition', *La Nef*, September 1964, 41–7. A lucid analysis of the meaning of racism, distinguishing it from nationalism.

SEGAL, R., *The Race War*, Penguin Books, 1967. A remarkable survey of race relations around the world by a neo-Marxist, but slightly marred by a view of the causes of racialism which is too narrowly confined to simple economic factors, and thus minimizing other social and psychological factors.

SIMPSON, G. E. AND YINGER, J. M., *Racial and Cultural Minorities*, Harper & Row, 1965. Possibly the best eclectic analysis of race relations.

THOMPSON, E. T. AND HUGHES, E. C., *Race: Individual and Collective Behaviour*, Collier-Macmillan, 1965. A useful collection of readings with a thorough bibliography. Makes a valuable supplement to Simpson and Yinger.

3. *Race relations – some major theoretical analyses*

BANTON, M., *Race Relations*, Tavistock Publications, 1967. A solid and comprehensive account, somewhat deficient in psychological discussion.

COX, O. C., *Caste, Class and Race*.

FRAZIER, E. F., *On Race Relations*. University of Chicago Press, 1968. Although focused on the problems of American blacks, Frazier was a pioneer in the theoretical analysis of race relations as a student of social change.

REX, J., *Race Relations in Sociology Theory*, Wiedenfeld & Nicholson, 1970. A fresh analysis from a neo-Marxist point of view of race relations, that goes far beyond insipid and tentative descriptive studies, and creates a body of significant analytical tools.

VAN DEN BERGHE, P. L., *Race and Racism – a Comparative Perspective*, John Wiley, 1968.

4. *Race differences*

KLINEBERG, O., *Social Psychology*, Holt, Rinehart & Winston, 1962. Although in need of revision to incorporate more recent material, this is the clearest introductory account of the significance of race differences to intelligence, personality, etc. It is still the best account of 'the social factors in human nature'.

PASAMANICK, B., 'Some sociobiologic aspects of science, race, and racism', *Amer. J. Orthopsychiatry*, 1969, **39**, 1, 7–15. A presidential address to the American Psychopathological Association, this paper reviews the issues of racial differences.

DREGER, R. M. AND MILLER, K. S., 'Comparative psychological studies of Negroes and Whites in the USA: 1960–1965', *Psychological Bulletin Monograph Supplement*, 1968, **70**, 3 (2), 1–58. An invaluable and comprehensive review.

5. *Attitude formation and attitude change*

ALLPORT, G. W., *The Nature of Prejudice*, Doubleday, 1958. A slightly shortened version of the classic social psychological study of prejudice.

BETTELHEIM, B. AND JANOWITZ, M., *Social Change and Prejudice*, Collier-Macmillan, 1965. A sociological and psychoanalytical analysis of how social threat and insecurity lead to an increase in individual insecurity and group hostility.

ADORNO, T. W. *et al.*, *The Authoritarian Personality*, John Wiley Science Editions, 1964. A highly influential study of the family, social and psychological make-up of prejudiced and unprejudiced people.

CLARK, K. B., *Prejudice and Your Child*, Beacon, 1963. How do children learn about race? What can be done about it?

CLEAVER, E., *Soul on Ice*, Cape 1969. A collection of essays by an American black, many with brilliant insight and all searingly polemical, about the psychological consequences of contemporary racial clash.

DICKS, H. V., 'Personality traits and National Socialist ideology', *Human Relations*, 1950, **3**, 111–54. A modified Freudian approach to attitude formations: how does the social atmosphere of the family condition political attitudes and ideology?

FANON, F., *The Wretched of the Earth*, Penguin, 1970. An African psychiatrist's description of the effects of a racist colonialism on the personalities of the colonizers and the colonized. Impressionistic, it has, despite its selected evidence, profoundly influenced the black power-black-identity movements in the USA and elsewhere.

GOODMAN, M. E., *Race Awareness in Young Children*, Collier-Macmillan, 1964. A research study of the onset of racial consciousness among infants, and of its damaging results to the personalities of 4-year olds.

HARDING, J. *et al.*, 'Prejudice and Ethnic Relations', in Lindzey, G. and Aronson, E., *The Handbook of Social Psychology*, vol. 5, Addison–Wesley, 1969. A major review article.

MALCOM X WITH HALEY, A., *The Autobiography of Malcom X*, Hutchinson, 1966.

MCGUIRE, W. J., 'The nature of attitudes and attitude change', in Lindzey, G. and Aronson, E., op. cit., vol. 3.

SHELTON, A. J., 'The Black mystique: Reactionary extremes in négritude', *African Affairs*, 1964, **63,** 251, 115–28

SHERIF, M., 'Experimental and field research: Man in in-group and inter-group relations', in, Sherif, M., *Social Interaction*, Aldine Press, 1967. Demonstrates how inter-group relations can be methodically manipulated to change individual attitudes of group members.

WILLIAMS, R. M., *Strangers Next Door*, Prentice-Hall, 1964. A study of group co-operation and conflict, which shows that prejudice is reduced by equal-status contact.

6. *Great Britain*

Most studies of race relations in Great Britain have been restricted to specific issues and to particular social problems, and no adequate general survey was published until the Institute of Race Relations published in 1969 its overall survey of race relations in Britain, based upon commissioned research. The following give a comprehensive overview, which should be supplemented by current articles in *Race*, *Race Today* and the *Race Relations Bulletin* of the Runnymede Trust. The Institute of Race Relations publishes many fact papers.

(a) *General*

HOOPER, R. (ed.), *Colour in Britain*, BBC, 1965. A useful introductory survey.

ROSE, E. J. B. *et al.*, *Colour and Citizenship*, OUP, 1969. The most comprehensive account of race problems in the British Isles, with a chapter of policy recommendations. A shortened version, brought up to date and with a slightly different political emphasis is Deakin, N. *et al.*, *Colour, Citizenship and British Society*, Panther Modern Society, 1970.

WOLSTENHOLME, G. E. W. AND O'CONNOR, M. (eds.), *Immigration-Medical and Social Aspects*, Churchill, 1966.

(b) *The major official statements include:*

Immigration from the Commonwealth, H.M.S.O., 1965, Cmnd. 2739.

The Problems of Coloured School-Leavers, H.M.S.O., 1969, 413–1, 2, 3, and 4.

Council Housing: Purposes, Procedures and Priorities, H.M.S.O., 1969.

Report of Race Relations Board, 1968–9, H.M.S.O. (annually).

(c) *Education and youth*

BURGIN, T. AND EDSON, P., *Spring Grove – the Education of Immigrant Children*, OUP, 1967.

MILLER, H., *Race Relations and the Schools in Great Britain*, Phylon, 1966, **27**, 3, 247–67.

The Problems of Coloured School-Leavers, op. cit.

Immigrants and the Youth Service, H.M.S.O., 1967.

(d) *Discrimination*

DANIEL, W. W., *Racial Discrimination in England*, Penguin Books, 1968.

FOOT, P., *Immigration and Race in British Politics*, Penguin Books, 1965.

HEPPLE, B., *Race, Jobs and the Law in Britain*, Penguin Books, 1970.

MCPHERSON, K. AND GAITSKELL, J., *Immigrants and Employment: two case studies in East London and in Croydon*, Institute of Race Relations, 1969.

STREET, H. *et al.*, *Anti-Discrimination Legislation*, P.E.P., 1967. An excellent report (not followed in the Race Relations Act, 1968) on (1) the scope of English law on discrimination; (2) the laws in some other countries and (3) a consideration of how the law might be better used as an instrument of social policy.

WRIGHT, P. L., *The Coloured Worker in British Industry*, OUP, 1968.

ZUBAIDA, S. (ed.), *Race and Racialism*, Tavistock, 1970.

(e) *Studies of areas and other problems*

BAGLEY, C., *Social Structure and Prejudice in Five English Boroughs*, I.R.R., 1970.

BLOOM, L., *Familiar Strangers – a Study of Black and White Settlement in Cardiff* (forthcoming), I.R.R.

BROWN, *The Unmelting Pot – an English Town and its Immigrants*, Macmillan, 1970.

BURNEY, E., *Housing on Trial – a Study of Immigrants and Local Government*, OUP, 1966.

DESAI, R., *Indian Immigrants in Britain*, OUP, 1964.

GLASS, R. AND POLLINS, H., *Newcomers – the West Indians in London*, Allen & Unwin, 1960.

LAMBERT, J. R., *Crime, Police and Race Relations: a study in Birmingham*, OUP, 1970.

LITTLE, K. L., *Negroes in Britain: a Study of Racial Relations in English Society*, Kegan Paul, 1947. The classic study of a settled 'immigrant' area, Cardiff. Despite its age is well worth studying for its blending of anthropological methods with historical and political skill.

NGKWEE CHOO, *The Chinese in London*. OUP, 1968.

PATTERSON, S., *Dark Strangers: a Study of West Indians in London*, Tavistock, 1963; abridged, Penguin Books, 1965. An early study of Brixton, using impressionistic anthropological methods, but illustrating problems of acculturation.

REX, J. AND MOORE, R., *Race, Community and Conflict – a Study of Sparkbrook*, OUP. A study of housing and urban change in the city of Birmingham, which combines empirical investigation with an attempt to formulate a theory of race relations.

7. *South Africa*

The general situation is best summarized in two annual volumes: (i)

HORRELL, M. (ed.), *A Survey of Race Relations in South Africa*, S.A. Institute of Race Relations, Box 97, Johannesburg. A detached review of events, which rarely allows its objectivity to be affected by the liberal views of the Institute; (ii) *State of South Africa: Economic, financial and statistical year book*, Da Gama Publishers, Johannesburg. An exhaustive compilation, invaluable, provided that its conservative politics are regarded cautiously.

The historical background, which is almost more important in South Africa than in the USA, is presented conveniently in:

MACCRONE, I. D., *Race Attitudes in South Africa*, University of the Witwatersrand, 1965. Although first published in 1937, this study is still only partly dated, and remains the most detailed and comprehensive study of the development of race attitudes, combining the approaches of history, experimental and social psychology.

RHOODIE, N. J. AND VENTER, H. J., *Apartheid – a Socio-historical Exposition of the Origin and Development of the Apartheid Idea*, de Bussy, 1960. A conventional and conservative view, that minimizes the irrational elements.

VATCHER, W. H., *White Laager – the Rise of Afrikaner Nationalism*, Pall Mall, 1965.

SIMONS, H. J. AND R. E., *Class and Colour in South Africa 1850–1950*, the most distinguished analytical history of modern South Africa.

WILSON, M. AND THOMPSON, L., *The Oxford History of South Africa – South Africa to 1870*, OUP, 1969, an interesting review of early history that seeks to analyse the relations with one another of the many groups in South Africa, and is particularly sensitive to the economic factors in group conflict.

Sociological or political apologetics for *apartheid* or against it, are innumerable, and include:

HOLLOWAY, J. E., *The problems of Race Relations in South Africa*, South African Information Services. Compare with:

PATON, A., *The Long View*, Pall Mall, 1968 (a liberal approach), and with *The Road to South African Freedom*, South African Communist Party, n.d.

On the problems of urbanization and industrialization, basic references are:

KUPER, L., *An African Bourgeoisie*, Yale University Press, 1965. Wider in scope than its title suggests, this study (based in part on interviews) probes the psychological and social effect of *apartheid* upon the slowly growing class of middle-class Africans.

MBEKI, G., *South Africa: the Peasant's Revolt*, Penguin, 1965, presents an account in sharp contrast with the official: *Report of the Commission for the socio-economic development of the Bantu areas*, Government Printer, Pretoria, UG No. 61/1955. (The Tomlinson Report.)

VAN DEN BERGHE, P. L., *South Africa – A Study in Conflict*, Wesleyan University Press, 1965. A sociological analysis of the economic, political and social tensions generated by *apartheid*.

Race and inter-ethnic attitudes in South Africa have been studied intensively for at least as long as in the USA. A useful general account is by Mann, J. W., 'Attitudes towards ethnic groups', in Adam, H. (ed.), *Social change in South Africa*, Munich, Piper-Verlag, forthcoming.

Other references include:

BIESHEUVEL, S., 'The measurement of African attitudes towards European ethical concepts, customs, law and administration of justice', *J. Nat. Inst. Personnel Research,* Johannesburg, 1955, **6,** 5–17.

BIESHEUVEL, S., 'Further studies on the measurement of attitudes towards western ethical concepts'. *J. Nat. Inst. Pers. Res.,* 1959, **7,** 141–55.

BLOOM, L., 'Some psychological concepts of urban Africans', *Ethnology,* 1964, **3,** 1, 66–96.

DANZIGER, K., 'The psychological future of an oppressed group, *Social Forces,* 1963, 42, 31–40.

DOOB, L. W., 'Psychology', in Lystad, R. A. (ed.), *The African World,* Praeger, 1965. A systematic, annotated account of a wide range of research.

HUDSON, W. *et al., Anatomy of South Africa,* Purnell (Johannesburg), 1966. An interesting account, based on interviews and surveys, of white race attitudes by three white psychologists.

LEVER, H., 'An experimental modification of social distance in South Africa. *Human Relations',* 1965, **18,** 149–54.

MACCRONE, I. D., 'Reaction to domination in a colour-caste society: a preliminary study of the race attitudes of a dominated group', *J. Social Psychology,* 1947, **26,** 69–98.

MORSBACH, H. AND G., 'Attitudes of South Africans towards various national and racial groups', *International J. Psychology,* 1967, **2,** 4, 289–97.

PETTIGREW, T. F., 'Personality and sociocultural factors in intergroup attitudes: a cross-national comparison', *J. Conflict Resolution,* 1958, **2,** 29–42. Still a topical source on the relative roles of psychological and sociocultural factors determining race attitudes.

8. The Americas

Still the classic general statement is Myrdal, G., *An American Dilemma,* McGraw-Hill, 1964 (first published, 1944), written from a liberal viewpoint. A short, but pregnant statement of the black point of view is Carmichael, S. and Hamilton, C. V., *Black Power,* Penguin Books, 1969, which although it has been surpassed in vehemence has rarely been equalled in cogency.

For the psychologist, the problem of identity is the crucial dilemma for American blacks, and though this cannot be divorced from political, economic and social problems, psychological analyses are essential.

BAUGHAM, E. E. AND DAHLSTROM, W. G., *Negro and White Children,* Academic Press, 1968. A detailed empirical study, educational and psychological, of a comparable sample of black and white children, their disadvantages and their strengths.

ESSIEN-UDOM, E. U., *Black Nationalism – a Search for Identity in America,* Penguin, 1968. A political scientist examines the early history of black nationalism.

KVARACEUS, W. C., *Negro Self-concept: Implications for School and Citizenship.* McGraw-Hill, 1965. An invaluable analysis of the psychological and educational consequences of being black.

PETTIGREW, T. F., *A Profile of the Negro American,* van Nostrand, 1954. The most comprehensive psychological account of what it means to be black.

Accounts that are more psychoanalytical than psychological in their type of research approach are:

DOLLARD, J., *Caste and Class in a Southern Town*, Anchor Books, 1957.

ERIKSON, E. H., *Childhood and Society*, Penguin, 1965.

Identity-Youth and Crisis, Norton, 1968.

KOVEL, J., *White Racism – a Psychohistory*, Pantheon Books, 1970.

Some of the historical studies have added both to historical-sociological and psychological understanding, but should be supplemented by articles appearing in such periodicals as *American Journal of Orthopsychiatry, Psychiatry, Journal of Social Issues, Journal of Negro Education, Journal of Social Psychology, Phylon, Transaction*, which frequently deal with race relations problems with an empirical psychological or psychiatric emphasis.

A selection of major historical studies includes:

BOGGS, J., *Racism and the Class Struggle*, Monthly Review Press, 1970. An acute Marxist analysis, wider in scope than its title suggests.

ELKINS, S., *Slavery – a Problem in American Institutional and Intellectual Life*, Grosset & Dunlap, 1963, includes a chapter on 'Slavery and Personality'.

GENOVESE, E. D., *The Political Economy of Slavery – Studies in the Economy and Society of the Slave South*, MacGibbon and Kee, 1966.

The World the Slaveholders Made, Allen Lane, The Penguin Press, 1970.

These two studies by Genovese, often brilliant, always acute, demonstrate how the slave societies of the deep South contained the economic seeds of their ruin, and (by implication) suggest how this form of society entails its peculiar psychology – among slave owners as much as among slaves.

GOSSETT, T. F., *Race – The History of an Idea in America*, Schocken Books, 1965. An extraordinary analysis of an obsession.

JORDAN, W. D., *White over Black*, University of North Carolina Press, 1969. The most meticulously documented and ably analysed historical survey of modern USA.

More directly related to social-psychological considerations of the relationship of problems to solutions are the following – a few of an endlessly expanding library:

CRUSE, H., *The Crisis of the Negro Intellectual*, W. H. Allen, 1969. Analyses the dilemma of the American black who 'cannot even identify with the American nation . . . he is left in the limbo of social marginality', and critically examines the notion of 'integration'.

The Autobiography of Malcolm X, Penguin Books, 1969.

Malcolm X Speaks, Merit Publishers, New York, 1965.

Malcolm X better than any other writer has depicted the experience of the black man in the modern world, and has shown how social conditions cannot be radically altered unless individual personality also changes. Malcolm X compares interestingly with Fanon.

Report of the National Advisory Commission on Civil Disorders, Bantam Books, 1968. The most general account of racial tensions and possible methods of ameliorating them. Although written of the USA, many of the sections on 'What can be done?' are not irrelevant to situations elsewhere.

PASSOW, A. H., *Education of the Disadvantaged*, Holt, Rinehart and Winston, 1968. Far broader than its title suggests: essential reading.

Other parts of the Americas ought to be touched upon, if only for a picture of the contrasts in race relations situations. See, for example,

Brazil:

FREYRE, G., *The Masters and the Slaves*, Knopf, 1964.
WAGLEY, C. (ed.), *Race and Class in Rural Brazil*, UNESCO, 1952.
Amazon Town, a Study of Man in the Tropics. Macmillan, 1964.
Mexico:

LEWIS, O., *Five Families*, Wiley, 1962.
Tepoztlan – Village in Mexico, Holt, Rinehart & Winston, 1960.
The West Indies:

HENRIQUES, F., *Family and Colour in Jamaica*, Eyre and Spottiswoode, 1953.
LAMMING, G., *In the Castle of my Skin*, Longmans, 1970.
WILLIAMS, E., *Capitalism and Slavery*, André Deutsch, 1964.

Index of Names

Subject Index

Age, and race awareness, 42–6, 54–8, 109

Aggression, 157

Africans, 16, 17, 19–20, 21, 32–3, 35, 48, 54, 71, 73, 85–6, 90, 102, 146–7

Anti-Semitism, and demonic conspiracy myth, 36–7, 65, 80–1, 86–7, 113–17

Apartheid, 33, 35, 117, 137, 170–71

Arusha Declaration, 35

Aryan myth, 37–9

Attitudes, ch. 3 *passim*, and ideology, 26–7, 28–30, 31–2, 33; and the family, 60–5, 66–7; measurements of, 106–12; modificability, 154–9; South Africa, 82–3, 135–9

Black Muslims (also see Négritude, Identity) 53, 73, 76–7, 146, 170

Calvinist ideology, 35, 132, 134, 135

Caste, 29

Children (also see Family, and Attitudes) aggression, 65–6; racial awareness, 42–8; self-awareness, 48–54; 'defeated', 142–4

Civil Disorders, Report of the National Advisory Commission on, 191

Civil Rights, Report of Commission, 142

Colonization, attitudes, 33, 34, 69–79 (Mannoni), 86, 106–7, 133–4, 115 (GB)

Coloureds, South Africa, 119, 120

Commonwealth, immigration from, 187

Conflict, advantages of, 162–3

Contact, and education, 167–8; equal status, 163–5; residential, 165–7; situational and prejudice, 167

Culture, 18–20, 38, 68–73, 114, 129, 132–5, 137, 143, 162, 170

Dehumanization, 48, 54, 143–7

Doll play, 45–6

Economic factor in race relations, 28–30, 32, 33, 112, 118–19, 125–6, 133–4, 142

Education, and attitudes, 42–3, 137–9; and intelligence, 20–3, 24–5; and language skills, 143–4; in South Africa, 120–2; in USA, 142–3; Head Start, 24

Ethnocentricism, 59–60, 61–4

Family and race attitudes, 60–5

Fascists, British Union of, 113

France, 106–7

Genocide, 36–9

Germany, and Aryan myth, 38; and race ideology, 37–8

Ghetto, psychology of, 95, 148

Great Britain, background of race relations, 85–8; causes of race attitudes, 112–16; facts and figures, 88–93; racialism, prevalence of, 106–12; Cardiff, 97–106; Slough, 95–7; Sparkbrook, 93–5

Group differences in intellectual ability, 20; differences in personality, 23, 24–6, 68, 71–2

Housing, Council – purposes, procedures and priorities, 187; Cardiff, 98; Sparkbrook, 93–5; and race relations, 165–7